At Your Command

At Your Command

The remarkable story of
Reb Yechiel Mechel Rabinowicz,
talmid chacham, inventor, activist, philanthropist,
and — always — faithful Jew

Bracha Perel Toporowitch

TARGUM/FELDHEIM

First published 2003

ISBN 1-56871-243-x

Published by:
TARGUM PRESS, INC.
22700 W. Eleven Mile Rd.
Southfield, MI 48034
E-mail: targum@netvision.net.il
Fax: 888-298-9992
www.targum.com

Distributed by:
FELDHEIM PUBLISHERS
202 Airport Executive Park
Nanuet, NY 10954
www.feldheim.com

Printed in Israel

This book is dedicated to all of my teachers and mentors who enabled me to grow and develop and reach for my dreams. Starting all the way back with my father, *z"l,* and, *ybl"c,* my mother, *shetichyeh,* and my early teachers who guided me in life and right through the years to my later teachers, my dear husband, *n"y,* and all of my mentors who gave a little piece of themselves to me until this very day.

May Hashem enable us to continually learn and grow in Torah and spirituality and to fulfill our *tafkid* in life.

Acknowledgments

Firstly, to You, Hashem, for giving me the capabilities necessary for producing this work, I offer my praise and thanks. My prayer is that it will inspire others to connect to You with greater devotion, as I have been inspired time and time again while doing the research for it.

To the wonderful members of the Targum staff I wish to give my profound thanks. You worked so closely and patiently with me in producing the book just to my liking.

To all the dear people who contributed of your time to share with me your memories of my father, *z"l*, and to enable me to construct the flow of his life, my sincerest thanks.

And lastly, to my dear husband, *n"y*, and family, who tolerated my taxing writing schedule, my thanks are given from the bottom of my heart. Your support was invaluable to me, especially when the writing seemed endless. It was for you, my dears, that I wished to leave this legacy, so that you might know who your grandfather and great-grandfather was.

Contents

Preface

How does one tell a story about a very special and unique person? So many of my memories are seen through a child's eyes. How can I create a true picture of him when there is so much that I don't remember?

These are the thoughts that flood my mind as I contemplate the task I have set for myself: to write about the life and times of my father, Reb Yechiel Mechel Rabinowicz, *z"l*. How can the life of this man, great in so many ways, go forgotten? I want my children and grandchildren to know. I want my friends to know. I want the world to know.

And so, poor as the results may be, I take pen to paper and pray that I do justice to my father's memory.

One of my earliest memories of Deddy, as we called him with the London accent we picked up in our first home, was of him sitting on the couch pulled up to the table for the

Pesach seder, looking regal in his white *kittel.* Sometimes a male guest would be seated next to him on the couch. When one of us became really tired as the seder continued late into the night, we would drag ourselves over to the couch, curl up next to Father, and drop off to sleep. There was something very special about dozing off on the couch next to him on seder night.

My recollections of my father are not complete. I have tried to fill in the gaps to the best of my ability, relying on the tales my mother told us and the family traditions we heard and absorbed from so many different sources. Some of the stories I heard for the first time from various people during the *shivah.* Sometimes, in my recreation of the tales, I have used the exact words uttered by my father, *z"l,* or, *ybcl"c,* my mother's lips as they recounted their stories to me. Sometimes I've had to improvise, but I have tried to remain true to the emotions and moods of the incidents to the best of my ability. And some of the details I have filled in using my imagination in order to be able to describe the scene more vividly and make the book more readable. I also changed some names to protect their privacy; these I marked with an asterisk.

If I have done a less than fitting job of depicting the great person that my father was, I beg his forgiveness and that of my mother and siblings. I hope they all realize that my only desire is to do justice to the memory of a very special and inspiring Jew and a very special and inspiring father. May Hashem help me in my task.

Prologue

We had moved back to Eretz Yisrael recently and were celebrating our first Pesach in our newly built home in Zichron Yaakov. I thought this was a good opportunity to tell my married children, who were with us for *yom tov*, something of their grandfather. When I asked them what they remembered about their *zeidy*, they had their own stories to tell. My daughter Chany asked me, "Ima, why don't you write a book about Zeidy?" I had been thinking of doing just that, ever since he passed away seven years earlier, but I had never gotten around to actually starting the project.

That Pesach my daughter planted the idea in my mind that "I am really going to write this book." Immediately after Pesach I got started.

I took out the box of tapes. There were tapes of people speaking at the *shivah*. There were tapes of my mother talking about my father, which I had recorded several years earlier, and tapes my nephew had recorded while in conversation with her. I decided to begin with those.

I inserted one of the cassettes into the tape recorder and took a deep breath as I pressed the Play button. Suddenly I was transported through time and space, to war-torn Europe of over half a century ago.

"The Chap Is All Right"

It was autumn, and the leaves were turning brilliant colors. The year was 1942, and England was deeply embroiled in the war. The bombs fell relentlessly on British soil, while Britain struggled desperately to release itself from the Nazi stranglehold.

My father and mother had spent Rosh HaShanah in the little village where they slept at night. They could not sleep at home. Birmingham, the large industrial city where they lived, was being bombed heavily, especially at night.

There was a chill in the air as my father left Birmingham on his way to his room in the village. The clouds were gathering, and it looked like rain. He drove along the road, watching the shadows grow longer as the sun merged into the horizon. It was fast turning dark.

My father had not been able to say *Tashlich* on Rosh HaShanah, so he scanned both sides of the road, looking for a body of water in which to "throw away his sins." This was his last opportunity to say the *Tashlich* prayer before Hoshana Rabbah.

Soon he came across a little park. Deep within he made out a lake. Joyfully he stopped the car on the side of the road and ran through the gate of the park to the water. It started raining, but that did not stop him. My father immersed himself in the *Tashlich* prayer, becoming oblivious to his surroundings. He whispered the words of his prayers fervently, begging Hashem not only to save him but all of *klal Yisrael.*

Finally, he finished and turned to leave, with hope in his heart that Hashem would answer his pleas. He walked toward the gate and stopped in shock. The entrance gate to the park was locked for the night! He walked along the fence, looking for a way out. He hadn't been searching long before he was accosted by a park guard.

"Hey, you! What are you doing there? Come with me!"

He wasn't given a chance to explain before he found himself at the police station. My father was often suspected of being a German spy, because he looked "different." Englishmen did not grow beards in those days, and my father's beard and chassidic garb caught people's attention. This and his foreign accent aroused suspicion.

The police searched him and the car thoroughly for a bomb. Once they were satisfied that he would not blow them up, they began interrogating him.

"What were you doing in the park?" they asked.

"I was praying."

"Praying! In this rain? Are you mad, praying in the middle of a storm? Why didn't you pray in the church? Or in your house?" they asked incredulously.

"Because," he said, "outside, amid nature, one feels closer to God."

They looked at him in amazement. His straightforward, nonapologetic manner convinced them.

"You know, the chap is right! We ought to learn from him."

My father took advantage of the change in tone and took the offensive.

"What's going on here? I work for the government, and this is the way you treat me?"

He gave them the phone numbers of various government ministers for whom he supplied war materials. They made the calls and verified that "the chap is all right."

"Okay, sir, you're fine. You can pray wherever you feel like. Keep on praying for us." They escorted him out of the police station and watched him drive off.

Who was this man who was not intimidated by the police? Who impressed others as an individual of integrity and holiness?

This was my father.

The Early Years

My father was born in the small town of Skolye, Poland on May 1, 1910. He was the sixth child in a family of nine, the third son. He was named Yechiel Mechel after the famed Zlochover Maggid, one of the family ancestors. His father, Reb Boruch Pinchas, was a chassidic Rebbe, the founder of the Skolyer dynasty, son of the holy tzaddik Reb Eliezer Chaim, and seventh generation from the famed Ba'al Shem Tov, founder of the chassidic movement.

My grandfather, the Skolyer Rebbe, was a tremendous *talmid chacham*; most of his days were spent delving in Torah. He was known to have performed many miracles in his short life of forty-six years. It is told that he exorcized a dybbuk from a demented woman in front of the Jewish community in the town shul, and my father knew an elderly man in Boro Park who had been witness to this miracle.

Rabbi Mattisyah Friedman, the Shtefeneshter Rebbe, my step-great-grandfather

My great-grandfather, the holy Reb Eliezer Chaim from Yampela, Russia

My grandfather Reb Boruch Pinchas Rabinowicz, the holy Skolyer Rebbe, in Vienna

My grandmother Rebbetzin Chaya Udel Brocha Rabinowicz, in Vienna

My grandfather Reb Avigdor Schorr from Romania

My grandmother Bluma Raizel Schorr

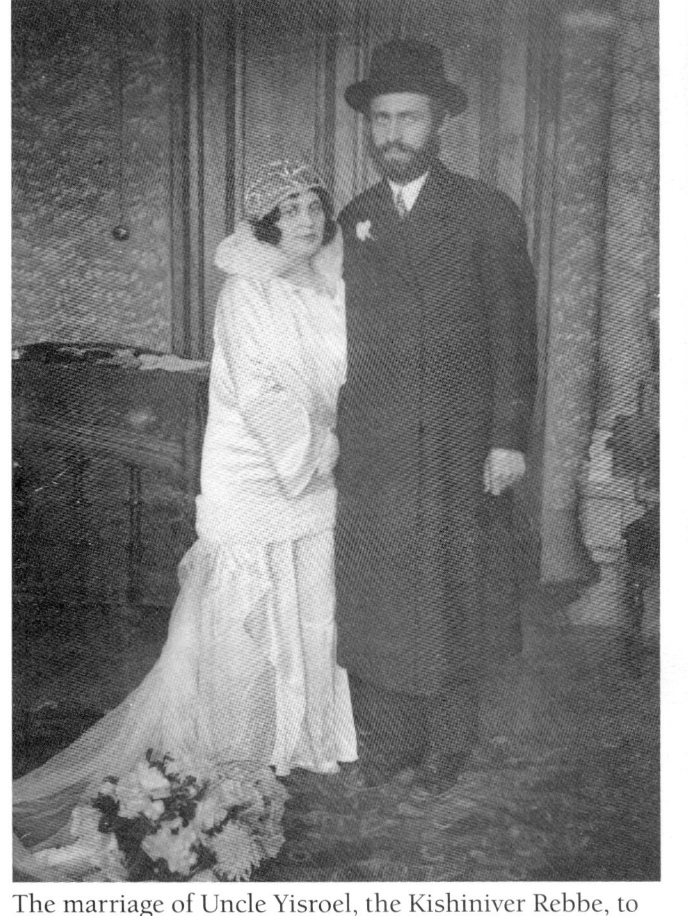

The marriage of Uncle Yisroel, the Kishiniver Rebbe, to Suranu Twersky (Mother's aunt) in Romania

Right to left: Father, his brother Reb Yisroel, and a cousin; seated: Father's brother Reb Dovid Yitzchok Isaac, in Vienna

Left to right, standing: Father, Gittele, Surale, her husband, Rav Aharon Arak; seated: Perele, Reb Yisroel's wife Suranu, and Reb Yisroel, in Vienna

Left: the *ohel* of the Skolyer rebbe; right: the *ohel* of Rabbi Yosef Engel; my grandmother Rebbetzin Chaya Udel Brocho in between, in Vienna

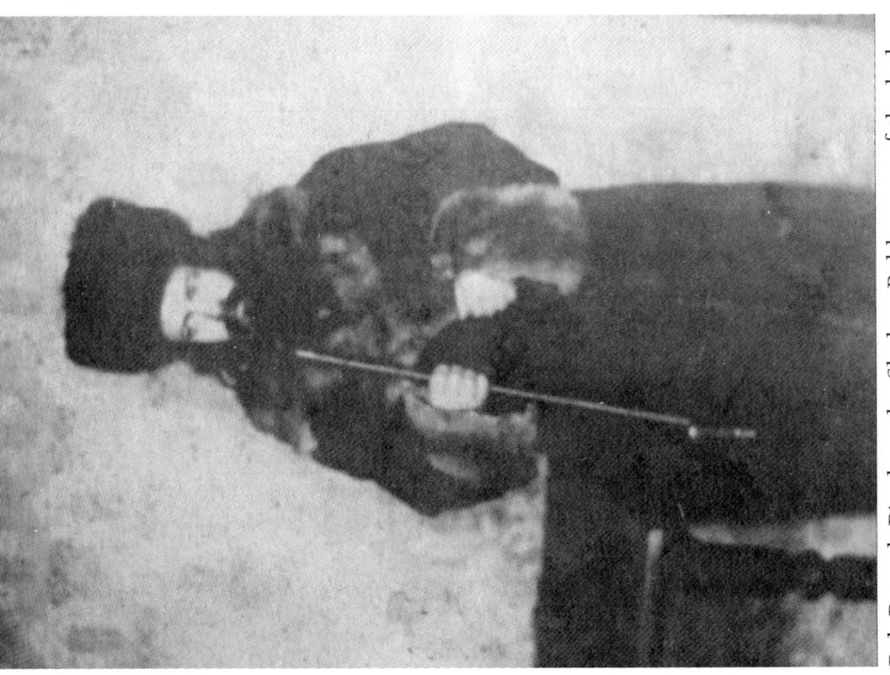

Reb Boruch Pinchas, the Skolyer Rebbe, son of the holy Reb Eliezer Chaim, in Vienna

Father, in Vienna

Mother, in London

Father, in Vienna

Father, in Jerusalem

My father's mother was Chaya Udel Brocha Rubin, the daughter of Reb Asher Yeshayah of Kolbisov in Poland.

My father was a precocious child. At his father's *tisch* at *seudah shelishis*, the chassidim would lift him up onto the table and ask him, a child of eight, to "tell them Torah," to give them his original insights on a Torah subject. As he grew in Torah knowledge, he was considered the greatest *masmid* in the family.

My father never went to school. He learned by himself at home, focusing exclusively on Torah studies. Compulsory schooling through the teen years was the law of the land in Austria. Parents who defied the law risked imprisonment. But my father suffered from detached retinas in both eyes, and his vision was very poor. As a result, he was exempt from attending public school. Most of his life he learned alone, without the benefit of teachers or study partners. Occasionally he tried learning with a *chavrusa*, a study partner, but soon realized that this system of learning was not beneficial for him, and he discontinued the partnership.

At the age of fifteen my father began davening *shacharis* for the congregation in his father's shul. He took over for his brother Reb Yisroel when Reb Yisroel married and moved to Romania. Forever after, almost to the year of his passing, wherever he lived in various communities in Europe, United States, and Israel, my father always found himself a minyan where he could daven *shacharis* on the *Yamim Nora'im*. This was a legacy he was not prepared to part with, for it states in the halachah that someone who is given the privilege of davening for the congregation on the *Yamim Nora'im* should not stop doing so.

The tunes of my father's davening have become so etched into my memory that I find it hard to daven any other way. It is years since I left home, yet when I daven in shul on the *Yamim Nora'im*, I still hum my father's *niggunim* to myself. These tunes, which I haven't heard for so many years, still have the ability to inspire me. No, it is more than that. It is the emotion and devotion that my father injected into his davening that can still rouse me to greater levels of inspiration.

A Miraculous Escape

My father's childhood years were a time of political upheaval. They were to leave him orphaned of both parents at a young age, and these years would act as a catalyst in the process of forming his character into a fiercely independent fighter.

During the First World War, his father, the Rebbe, went with my father's oldest brother, Reb Dovid Yitzchok Isaac, and his wife to Russia to help their fellow Jews. Wishing to avoid army service, Jews lined up by the hundreds for the Rebbe's *berachah*, and many of these Jews did manage to get out of military service.

The authorities looked upon the Rebbe as a nuisance and insurgent. He was warned by his followers to return home immediately, but he refused to leave the Yidden that looked to him for their salvation. The Rebbe and Reb Dovid Yitzchok Isaac were imprisoned for "anti-communist activities," and Reb Dovid Yitzchok Isaac's young wife was killed trying to escape. No one knew what had become of the Rebbe and his son.

While all of this was transpiring, it happened that one *erev Shabbos*, when my father was three years old, the

Rebbetzin Chaya Udel Brocha had a dream. Her mother appeared to her and told her to flee for her life. She was galvanized into action. She took the children and a few meager belongings and ran until she came to a village of Jews where she found refuge. Later she found out that her town had been ravaged by Cossacks, and she had escaped just in time. The Rebbe's chassidim helped her resettle in Budapest, Hungary, but Rebbetzin Chaya Udel Brocha had no idea what had happened to her husband and son and whether she would ever see them again.

In a miraculous manner Reb Boruch Pinchas and his son were released from jail, and in an equally miraculous manner they were reunited with his family in Budapest. What is so amazing about this part of the story is that although Russia was at war with Austro-Hungary, the prison authorities escorted the newly released "spies" over the Hungarian border.

Vienna

Eventually the family resettled in Vienna. Anti-Semitism was rampant, but amazingly the saintly Rebbe was left unmolested. He was able to find lodgings, with room for a shul, at Gross Stadtgutgasse 17, and soon gathered a very large group of loyal followers.

His holiness was apparent, even up until the time of his passing. On Shavuos, less than a year before his *petirah*, he indicated that his wife would be left a young widow. On Shabbos *parashas Tetzaveh* of the next year, he announced, "*Ich hob ahn einladenung* — I have an invitation." During the *melaveh malkah* on *motza'ei Shabbos*, he sang and danced with his chassidim much more than usual, full of health, vigor, and joy. Two weeks later he contracted virulent influenza, a victim of an epidemic in Europe after World War I.

In the hospital, though semiconscious, he refused to drink the milk the children tried to spoon into his mouth. He would allow only *chalav Yisrael,* milk that had proper Jewish supervision from the time of the milking, to pass his lips. Once, when the *chalav Yisrael* did not arrive on time, his son Reb Dovid Yitzchok Isaac thought that since the situation was one of *pikuach nefesh,* a matter of life and death, he could give his father the hospital milk. But before he was able to do so, his father opened his eyes and said, "*Chalav akum vilst du geiben dein Tatten? — Chalav akum* you want to give your father?"

A few days later the holy Rebbe was gone. The *rebbetzin* was left to fend for herself during that unsettling time following the war. My father was nine years old in that year of 1919. Reb Dovid Yitzchok Isaac, at twenty-one years of age, took upon his shoulders the mantle of leadership of the Skolyer dynasty. As young as he was, he proved to be a faithful leader of his flock.

And my father, he took upon himself the responsibility of supporting the family.

The Man of the Family

Life was fraught with danger and poverty. My father's eldest brother, Reb Dovid Yitzchok Isaac, the second Skolyer Rebbe, remarried and moved into his own home. His second wife was a Landau, a descendant of the Noda BiYehudah. Reb Yisroel married and moved to Kishinev, Romania, and was now known as the Kishinever Rebbe. My father's two older sisters were married and on their own. It was left to my father to support his mother and unmarried sisters, Perele, Gittele, Malkele, and Telchele.

Skolyer chassidim in one of the nearby towns might have happily crowned my father as their Rebbe — they had always expected him to become one. When my father was a child, everyone who knew him could see his deep love for learning. Even after his father passed away, and there was no one to guide him in his Torah studies, he could always be seen in some corner learning and always had a *sefer* with him. The chassidim were sure that "*Mechele vet zein de grester Rebbe* — Mechele will be the greatest Rebbe." But my father didn't much like the idea of being a Rebbe. He wanted to support himself by the toil of his own hands; he did not like to take handouts.

He could have become a *rav*, a *posek* who could judge in matters of halachah, a commendable and honest profession. My father's brother-in-law Rav Aharon Arak once wrote in an official document, after testing my father to ascertain his current Torah knowledge, "He is capable of accepting any rabbinical position in a Jewish community, and he will become a decided asset to any Jewish congregation that will choose him as their spiritual leader." But again, this meant he would be earning a livelihood from his Torah learning, something that was totally antithetical to his philosophy of life. This principle was apparent in the way he conducted his affairs until the very end.

His sense of responsibility and dedication to the family was amazing and expressed itself in numerous incidents throughout his life. As difficult as it was for such a young person, my father willingly became the man of the family. He was the doer, and if something had to be taken care of, "Mechele" was called upon to do it.

It was not easy. My father did not have a strong constitution. When he was sixteen years old, he was hospitalized with a high fever. The doctors were very concerned that this illness would affect his heart. The head professor of the hospital, in response to the seriousness of his condition, forbade my father to leave his bed.

It was during that time that his mother, the Rebbetzin Chaya Udel Brocha, passed away. The doctors, fearing for his health, did not permit the family to tell young Mechele the news. But someone innocently visited him at the hospital to be *menacheim avel,* to give comfort to the mourner, and so he discovered his bitter loss.

Eventually my father was transferred to another hospital where the doctors encouraged him to engage in physical activity and to build up his strength. Slowly he regained his health and, once again, was able to function as the active person that he was and resume the yoke of responsibility for his family. This feeling of responsibility remained with him throughout his life. As long as he was actively able, he was involved with the financial support of his siblings.

When my father's sister Perele, his senior by two years, was old enough to marry, he took upon himself the responsibility to contact *shadchanim.* The custom of the time was to give *nadin,* a dowry, for the bride, and therefore money was an issue. When a suitable proposal came along, and my father felt that it was a fitting match for his sister, he himself arranged to pay the promised dowry in installments. With that settled, he set up the meeting between the prospective bride and groom, Aharon Moshe Leifer, son of the Rebbe of Chust.

Perele traveled with my father and her brother, the Kishinever Rebbe, to meet the family in Hungary. She felt frightfully alone. After all, she was without a mother or father to accompany her at this most critical time in her life. That night, in the hotel they were staying in, she cried herself to sleep. She dreamed that her father and mother appeared to her.

Her father said, "Perele, you think you are alone. We are here with you. We are going along with you to see the *chasan*, and we are taking care of you. If you don't believe me, then look at this."

Her father opened a door. Behind the door was a young chassid with long *peyos*. "Here is your *chasan*."

When she awoke, she knew she was not alone. Later that day she met the prospective *chasan* — the young man she had seen in her dream. Perele became engaged to the young man.

In this and in many other ways, the family felt that their holy parents were watching out for them from Heaven.

When my father entered the business world, he remained devoted to his Torah studies. He brought a *sefer* with him wherever he traveled. No matter how late it was, he would never forego his learning. He set up for himself a rigorous program that included the study of *Chumash*, Gemara, all of his father's *sefarim*, the Rambam's writings, *Sefer HaMitzvos*, *Zohar*, Mishnah, *Shelah*, *Reishis Chochmah*, *Tur*, *Shulchan Aruch*, and *Minchas Chinuch*. For many years, he completed all of the Mishnah and the entire *Zohar* annually.

Only the most dire of circumstances would cause my father to miss a day of learning. He had a role model in his own father. My *zeide* immersed himself in learning most of the day and night. My father told us that he remembers how his father would place his feet in a bowl of freezing water in the late hours of the night so that he would not fall asleep while learning. It was said of him that he slept only two hours in a twenty-four-hour period. In his short life, my grandfather published many volumes of Torah insights and *sifrei Chassidus*. This was the fiery love of Torah and dedication to learning that my father inherited.

My father's first endeavor at earning a living was working for an insurance firm selling life insurance. He also taught himself law and wrote his own contracts.

As a youth, my father was actually quite shy, but he was determined to overcome his shyness in order to be successful in business. He purchased a home-study course designed for this purpose. Apparently it helped him because he succeeded in his profession and did quite well.

But there was something about this line of work that disturbed him: it dealt with death. In those days, buying life insurance was looked upon as though someone was making a bet with the Angel of Death. It didn't take very long before he decided to make a living in other ways. Instead of taking advantage of people's fear of death, he would earn a livelihood by using the brilliance of his mind. He turned his intellect to producing inventions.

The Technical Genius

My father developed several inventions and had them patented. He worked together with an engineer and was constantly learning new things. He learned whatever he needed to know in order to succeed in his endeavors. This intellectual capacity was an outgrowth of the development of his mind from learning Talmud. Through learning on his own he had developed the acumen and analytical abilities to figure things out on his own.

One of his inventions was a brush that released water or perfumed hair tonic as it was passed through the hair. This was a great gadget for the style-conscious people of his time, and it was very popular. Another invention of his was an adjustable picture frame. One was able to fold in the sides to adjust the frame size according to need. Father's sister Malkele helped him promote this product. He also took out a patent on a baby bath made of plastic. In those days baby baths were made of metal and were heavy and unwieldy.

His biggest invention, created later on in his life, was a radio in the shape of a globe. He called it the "Emor Radio, the radio sensation of the world!" It was a beautiful chromium-plated globe with an equatorial tuning band. As one turned the globe, the radio picked up frequencies around the world. It was, in essence, an early model of a shortwave radio. One of these radios graced my father's study in our home in Boro Park and immediately attracted a visitor's attention. It was a striking piece, and the Museum of Modern Art wished to acquire a sample. Because of this invention Father was able to obtain a tourist visa to the United States after the war.

The Yiddishe Handles Schulle

Besides using his creativity on a personal level, my father used his phenomenal mind to benefit the community. In those anti-Semitic times, leading to the rise of the Nazi regime, Orthodox Jewish children living in Vienna were unable to learn a trade, since all trade or commercial schools conducted classes on Shabbos. My father decided to establish the Yiddishe Handles Schulle, a Jewish trade school that observed the sanctity of Shabbos.

It was difficult to obtain the required permits, since the government ministries were not exactly accommodating to the needs of the Jewish populace. My father even encountered some opposition from the Jews in his community. After all, he was an uneducated chassidic young man. They thought that it was necessary for one to be an educated and cultured person in order to head a project such as this.

Despite the opposition, my father pushed ahead with his plan and he succeeded. He was the administrator of the school but was unable to serve as its director since he had no official schooling or degrees. Someone else filled this role.

Father was very proud of this accomplishment; it served an important function in the community. His sister's son Chaim Shmuel Arak attended the school. He was a *talmid chacham,* and he continued with his Torah learning, but he thought it would be a good idea to learn a trade as well.

My father's older sister, Rifka Frankel, ran a part-time business in the school. She set up a big barrel in the courtyard. During breaks and lunchtime she sold her homemade pickles and bread-and-butter sandwiches. It was a good way to supplement her income.

My father needed financial support for the school and was always on the lookout for likely donors. When he started traveling in order to market his inventions, he made contact with Jews all over Europe. This provided him with the opportunity to tell them about the school and the important function it served. In this way he managed to collect donations for the school's upkeep.

My father also founded the Austrian-Palestinian Association. Its purpose was to engender public relations and commerce with Israel, still called "Palestine" at that time. But he could not pursue this for very long since the political situation was deteriorating rapidly.

Father told us a most amazing tale. On the night of the inauguration evening for his new trade school, his mother appeared to him in a dream. He described to her how the Minister of Education himself, along with other government officials, had attended the evening and praised the school highly.

"It was a great *kiddush Hashem,* a non-Jew coming and praising our Jewish school!" he told her excitedly.

She made a derisive motion with her hand. "*Loz op!* — Leave it be! *Se gurnisht* — It's nothing!"

"But, Mama," he insisted, "don't you see how important this is for the Jewish community? Even the goyim appreciate what I have done!"

Again she made a motion with her hand and told him to forget about it. "*Loz op* — Leave it be! *Gey avek* — Go away! Go away from here!" she entreated him.

He was resistant, explaining to her that he could not abandon the school. But she repeated her request until he acquiesced.

Upon awakening from the dream, he felt he had no choice but to listen to the words of his mother, who was communicating to him and watching out for him from another world. Shortly after that he went to London with his newest invention in hand. It was a gadget for preventing leakage of gas, a very desirable item. He obtained a tourist visa for both the United States and England for the purpose of promoting his invention. How he managed to get the visas in those precarious times is anyone's guess.

He decided that he would first go to England with his invention. His brother Yisroel, the Kishinever Rebbe, had by now relocated to London from Romania. My father made plans for his move as well. He returned to Vienna and gave over his beloved *handles schulle* to an associate and shortly after returned to London.

My father was the first to leave Vienna prior to the Nazi invasion, but each one of his siblings had unbelievable *siyatta diShmaya,* divine intervention, and managed to get out in time via Romania, Switzerland, and England. One sister was aided by the righteous gentile Raoul Wallenberg, and the Skolyer Rebbe managed to get a visa to the United States before the war.

My father had no idea what the future held in store for him. When the Nazis entered Vienna, one of the people on their list was Mechel Rabinowicz, founder of the Judische Handles Schulle. But they could not find him. He was already in London.

London

Life in London started a new phase in my father's life. The year was 1936, and my father was twenty-six years old. He was living temporarily with an aunt, Mrs. Lifshe Albert, his father's sister. But my father was a fiercely independent man who insisted on fending for himself. He could have become a Rebbe in London, but he was opposed to using his *avodas Hashem* for earning a livelihood. He didn't have many options since he did not know English and had no money. What he did possess was his deep and intense *bitachon* in Hashem and his very sharp mind.

My father also had his patented inventions. After learning some basic English, he sought out buyers. He offered his gadget for preventing gas leaks to the gas company, a government enterprise. They were very interested. It would save the government a lot of money and prevent inadvertent gas poisoning.

The man at the gas company told him, "Mr. Rabinowicz, as soon as I get the go-ahead from my supervisors, I'm going to place my order. This is an absolutely genius invention! The government is going to love it!"

My father waited eagerly for the order to come; he sorely needed some income, since, besides supporting himself, he was sending money to Europe to his sisters. But in the interim World War II broke out, and he received the disappointing news that, at that time, the government was not placing orders for anything outside the war effort.

The gas company was in possession of the plans and a sample of my father's invention. Some years later, after the war, the gas company installed it in buildings, but no one bothered to pay the inventor for it. Probably no one even remembered who he was.

The baby baths also turned out to be a disappointment. My father was sure that his bath would sell like hotcakes. He manufactured about a thousand units, anticipating that they would be sold in no time. Unfortunately, the war broke out, and the sales market went dead. No one was buying anything other than the absolute essentials. My father remained with all the baby baths, not knowing what to do with them. He pondered the problem until he came up with an idea. He contacted someone in Reykjavik, the capital of Iceland. After sealing the drain holes of the baths, he successfully sold them as little boats!

The Loan

Father was almost destitute at this point and desperately needed to earn some money. He had given half of his savings to a penniless sister of his brother-in-law Rav Arak, who had remained alone in Vienna. He feared that she had no one to help her out, that she was probably starving, and could not bear the thought.

My father was feeling very lost and forlorn. One night he had a dream. He saw a tall, strong man coming toward him. Father thought that he was Eliyahu HaNavi posing as a gentile. He called out to him, "*Racheim alai! Racheim alai* — Have mercy on me! Have mercy on me!" The man picked him up high and held him aloft. When my father awoke, he knew that he would be taken care of; now he would go "up" and succeed.

Despite the obstacles that arose, my father persevered in his efforts. Every once in a while he would conclude a business transaction. At one point he received notice of an incoming shipment of his brushes from the Czech production plant. In order to release the shipment from customs he was required to pay a tariff. It was not a large amount of money, but my father had nothing at all with which to pay it. Without the money for customs he would be unable to receive the goods and would not be able to finalize the sale.

None of my father's family or acquaintances were able to lend him the necessary funds. My father knew that if one needed money one could go to a bank for a loan. He davened that Hashem should help him succeed and entered the first bank he came across that day. It was one of the larger British banks, a branch of Barclay's Bank in London. He asked to speak to the manager and was shown into his office.

Although my father had a heavy accent and barely knew English, he had great presence and exuded confidence.

Shaking the man's hand, he said, "Good morning, Mr. Peterson.* Nice day today."

Mr. Peterson nodded in agreement. "Yes, indeed," and waited for my father to get to the point.

"Mr. Peterson, I have started a new business here and need money. I am asking you for a loan of two hundred English pounds sterling." He showed him the invoice from the customs office and a description of the contents of the shipment.

The bank manager studied the papers. "Well, sir, we can discuss a loan. What can you tell me about your credit status?"

My father answered that he had no credit status in England.

The manager laughed. "You are some character! Tell me, sir, on what basis should I provide you with a loan if you have no credit in this country?"

My father sat up and very seriously answered, "Upon my word of honor!"

Mr. Peterson was taken aback. He was a proper Englishman, the kind of person who always stuck to rules and regulations. He stared at the bearded Jew for a moment, and the nobility of the man standing before him struck home.

"Mr. Rabinowicz," he said finally, "I have been a bank manager for over thirty years. I never once had a situation where someone requested a loan without any credit. Without that it is impossible for me to allow the bank to grant you a loan."

My father rose and took his coat in his hands. "Well, if that's the case," he said, "I am sorry that I took up your valuable time." He turned to leave.

"Wait a minute!" Mr. Peterson said quickly. "You have

whetted my curiosity. I can't allow the bank to give you a loan, but you know what? You strike me as a truly honest individual, and I am willing to do something that in my wildest imagination I would never have done. I am willing to give you this loan from my personal funds."

Mr. Peterson took out his checkbook, wrote out a check in the desired amount, and gave it to the stranger in front of him.

My father shook the hand of his newfound benefactor warmly. He asked him when he wished the money returned. They set a date for several days later. My father reassured the manager that he had nothing to worry about, that he would be there with the money on the day they had set.

My father left the bank with profuse thanks in his heart to Hashem. He wasn't surprised at his good fortune. His reliance on Hashem had proven justified time and time again.

Years later my mother asked him how he had the courage to walk into a bank and ask for a loan without having any credit status. He told her that he hadn't been nervous in the least about doing it. He had davened sincerely that Hashem help him. He felt that if Hashem would answer his plea, that would be an indication to him that this was the right thing for him to do. If Hashem would refuse his plea, then that would be an indication to him that this was not the right thing for him to do, and he would look for a different way of obtaining funds. The moment he passed a bank he felt immediately that he had to take the risk and ask for a loan.

My mother wanted to know how he was able to speak to the manager with almost no knowledge of English. He said that he prepared in advance the few words he needed to know in order to be able to convey his message. And with this small *hishtadlus* he went ahead.

With the money from Mr. Peterson in hand, Father was able to conclude his business transaction, and soon he had the funds with which to repay his loan. On the day the bank manager had stipulated, he went to the bank to fulfill his promise. When my father entered the bank, Mr. Peterson approached him and extended his hand to my father.

"Mr. Rabinowicz," he said, "is it really you? You have no idea what you did to me. I have not been able to sleep since I gave you the loan."

"Why not, Mr. Peterson?" Father asked, astonished.

"Each night, and especially last night, I twisted and turned in bed, wondering if I had gone mad giving you my money. I wondered if I would ever see you again, let alone see you at the bank today. This morning I rushed to work to find out what would happen. I must say that I can hardly believe it. In all of the long years that I have been a bank manager, never have I encountered a man with such integrity."

My father handed over the money he owed. He offered to pay interest, but Mr. Peterson refused. "Oh no, sir," the manager told him, "you gave me more than I gave you. I gave you money, but you have given me faith in mankind."

My father thanked him for his kind words and wished him a good day. Mr. Peterson wished my father good luck and assured him that if he ever needed a reference attesting to his credit reliability, he should send the inquirers to him.

Who can assess the value of the *kiddush Hashem* that took place as a result of my father's integrity? This was in a time when the Nazis were screaming their anti-Semitic propaganda to the world and the outbreak of war was imminent.

Working for the Government

My father had a little bit of money now, and he started a new enterprise. He rented a tiny room containing a bed, a table, and a typewriter. He could not afford a telephone, but was able to receive calls on his landlord's phone. That was the extent of his material wealth. Here he slept and cooked for himself.

Since it was wartime, the government was looking for skilled people for the production of munitions. He hung a large sign outside his "office" stating that he produced supplies for the war effort. He typed up advertisements to put in the newspaper in which he offered his services in this area of expertise.

Father scanned the ads in the paper. The government urgently needed people with experience in engineering and other technical skills. My father had never spent a day of his life learning engineering or anything remotely connected to the type of knowledge he needed in order to be able to fit the requirements requested. But at the moment he had no other way of earning a living, and he knew he had to try something. Somehow he would master whatever it was that he needed to know.

One ad asked for technicians with very precise workmanship skills. They were needed for the production of extremely important munitions for the war effort. Father decided that he would answer this ad and offer the government his services.

He recognized the urgent tone of the advertisement and figured he would make a more positive impression by replying via telegram. He was so impoverished at the time that he was not even sure whether he had enough money to pay for the telegram. He had only sixteen shillings left in his pocket!

As he wrote out the text of his reply onto the telegram form in the post office he noticed a hundred-pound note sitting on the desk next to him. This was a nice amount of money in those days.

He picked it up and went over to the post-office teller and told him he had found some money. The teller told him to look for the owner. No one was there, and no one had been there when my father came into the post office. He waited a while, thinking that perhaps the owner of the bill would reappear to claim his loss. He waited long enough to know that the owner of the money was not aware of his loss and was not returning for it. According to the halachah, the money was his, since he had found it in a public place and there was no sign or symbol on it to make the owner identifiable.

He sent off the telegram using the money he had just found and pocketed the change. He now had another tangible sign that Hashem was looking out for him.

Soon after, he got a call in response to his telegram. The caller wanted an interview.

It was a cold, wintry day and snow was falling. Two tall imposing army officers arrived at my father's "office." He welcomed them in and offered them a hot drink. They declined and got straight to the point.

They took out several blueprints and gave them to my father to examine. My father had a little familiarity with reading blueprints since he had had blueprints made up for his inventions. They told him to choose one that he would like to start with. He chose one of the blueprints, not even sure of what it was since it was part of some larger machine. They asked him to study it. He looked at it as though he was studying its contents.

"Can you make us a sample of this machine part?" they asked.

"Certainly, gentlemen. It will be no problem. I can make you whatever it is that you need," Father answered without hesitation.

"Mr. Rabinowicz," one of the officers said, "I must inform you of the urgency and the importance of producing this part. It plays a vital role in our war effort. It can save up to 40 percent of the petrol normally used in tanks, which will save the government a great deal of money. We have already had many offers from different firms. I can consider you for the contract only if you respond with speed and efficiency. Please tell me, sir, how soon will it be before you can give us a sample for inspection?"

My father looked at the papers in his hands. He understood the contents of the blueprints exactly as he understood how to perform brain surgery. Although he had no knowledge of what making the part entailed, he gave them a date for two months hence. They were satisfied.

"How much will it cost us, sir?" they asked.

Once again, my father was completely in the dark as to what it would cost to produce the part, but he picked a figure.

"The part will cost you thirty pounds sterling," he said.

"Excellent, excellent, Mr. Rabinowicz! We have had quotes from other firms for quite a bit more than that! We wish to engage you for the job. And we will wait for your call letting us know when we can examine the sample, no later than two months from today."

"Certainly, gentlemen, certainly," he replied. "But I must ask you for an advance on the payment in order for me to produce the sample."

"Money is no problem whatsoever, Mr. Rabinowicz. How much do you want?"

He named a sum, which they gave him. They shook hands over the deal and left.

That day Father studied the blueprints for many long hours, sitting over them late into the night and into the next day. He agonized over the details of engineering the part. Finally he figured out what had to be done. It was an extremely intricate and precise piece of machinery, some of its parts measuring a thousandth of an inch.

Years later my mother looked at the blueprints. Although she had a university education, she said that she could not make heads or tails out of them. She could not imagine how my father had figured them out. He once told my mother that figuring out a page of Gemara was more complicated than deciphering a blueprint.

My father investigated methods of producing the part. He used the money the officers had given him to hire a taxi and make the rounds of the various factories in the area. Not all of the parts could be manufactured in the same plant. He contracted different firms to produce the different parts. The smaller factories were less busy than the larger ones, and they were able to meet his deadline. He discovered that the cost of producing the part would be about eight pounds, a little more than a quarter of the amount he had asked for it. If he could actually produce the piece, he would be able to set himself up for continued production.

Over the next two months he brought the many parts of the intricate piece of machinery to his place, ready to be assembled. He found a skilled technician to help him put together the sample and had it completed for inspection exactly when he said he would. Father brought the sample to a London address he had been directed to and presented it to one of the high-ranking army officers, General Storch.* The officer was very pleased.

"Mr. Rabinowicz, I am very impressed with your efficiency and reliability. I see that I can rely on you completely. I would like to order five thousand additional units. How soon can you have them ready?"

"I will make the first thousand pieces within three months. The rest of the order will take longer." They settled on a date for the completion of the order.

"I must warn you, Mr. Rabinowicz, that when the initial order will be ready for delivery, you must travel personally with the truck to the designated address outside London. You must promise me that you will not let the shipment out of your sight for even a moment. These items are exceedingly valuable to the war cause, and we cannot risk anything happening to them. Only if you agree to this condition can I place the order with you. Are you agreeable to my conditions?"

"I give you my word of honor, General. You can rest at ease. I will travel with the shipment and not let it out of my sight for even a minute. I understand the importance of these war materials, and I will keep them under constant surveillance," Father reassured him.

The general was satisfied. Again my father asked for advance payment, and unbelievably the general paid him the full amount right then. It was a huge amount of money.

On the day he had promised delivery of the order Father traveled by truck to the address he had been given far from London. He found the desired location, but the office was empty. There were three names on the office door. One was a nobleman, Lord Winston,* and the other two were army officers, General Storch, whom he had met, and General Grim.* He inquired and was informed that one of the officers had been sent away on a government mission. They did not know where the other army officer was. He asked whether someone knew Winston's or the other officer's home addresses. No one was able to provide him with any information. He was left with several thousand prepaid valuable items with no one to deliver them to.

He left a letter in the office mailbox and asked them to contact him immediately. Then he returned to London. My father never got a reply to his letter. He sent numerous letters to the officers' office address, but they were returned to him undelivered. The men seemed to have disappeared into thin air.

My father was in possession of a huge sum of money and had no way of returning it to its owners. He asked a *rav* what to do and was told that he could keep the money, the equivalent of about three hundred thousand dollars!

Why did the army officers give my father the order to begin with? Why would they entrust him with a top-secret document? My father was obviously a foreigner who spoke a broken English. Through *siyatta diShmaya,* his travel papers proclaimed him as "stateless." Had it stated that he was Polish, he would surely have been deported to Poland upon the outbreak of the war. Had it stated that he was from Austria, no government official would trust him. Spies were parachuting onto British soil from Germany all the time. But these officials never even asked to see my father's identification papers! He had no education, no credentials, no references, no work facilities, and he looked different, dressed as he was in the garb of an observant Jew.

All of this was obviously part of Hashem's "blueprint" for my father's life. The ways of Hashem are strange and wondrous. Once again Father felt the hand of Hashem.

Birmingham

Father relocated to Birmingham, a major industrial area that became a munitions center during the war. The days were very tense and full. There was a lot of tension not only because of the war but also because of financial strains.

With the money he had earned in the mysterious London deal, my father opened a small factory, a foundry for arms parts — screws, bolts, and rings. He called his firm "Quick Supply, Ltd.," an appropriate name since he was never late with his orders. Father managed, with his charisma and determination, to obtain orders from the various government ministries for supplying materials for the war effort.

What was so amazing about all of this was that he was not an expert on armaments, nor was he an engineer or a mechanic, but somehow he was able to produce these parts.

He studied blueprints of the machinery and the various parts that he was hired to produce. No matter how complicated they were, he always managed to figure them out. Not only was he able to sell his products, but he was able to convince the government authorities that they were the best and the cheapest available. And so, for the duration of the war, he became an employee of the government.

In no time my father gained the trust of the government officials who had hired him because of his dependability and efficiency. He was engaged for the manufacture of mechanical devices of the highest priority for the Admiralty, the Ministry of Supply, and the Ministry of Aircraft Production. After the war he was awarded recognition by all three ministries for excellence and perseverance in the war effort.

Men who were not working for the war effort in some capacity were drafted to the army. Often refugees were sent to outlying places such as Australia. My father was held in such high regard that he received permission from the War Office to exempt people from army service and to maintain their visitor's visas if he hired them to work in his factory for the war cause. He hired as many people as he could to save them from the bitter fate that befell many refugees.

Upon moving to Manchester, Rabbi Shmuel Sperber, better known to us as Uncle Shmuel (he had married my mother's sister), took a job with him as associate director. His job was to take the orders for various items. The Trisker Rebbe's youngest daughter, Runee, took a job with Father as a secretary. An old uncle of Father's, Mr. Albert, worked in the factory as well. At some point, even Reb Yisroel, the Kishinever Rebbe, would work at the factory. So on the shop floor were all these Rebbes and chassidim and *talmidei chachamim* trying to handle the machinery and tools, manufacturing the very fine component parts. As comic as the scene may have appeared, the situation was deadly serious.

Besides producing the small arms parts, the government contracted my father for production of munitions. Since he was incapable of actual production in his own plant, he placed his orders in various factories in Birmingham, London, and other industrial areas. He was held responsible for quality results and meeting deadlines.

One of the things that impressed Uncle Shmuel, a *rav* and *talmid chacham*, was that every day, no matter what happened, even when the War Office summoned him to their center, Father would learn for one hour. It didn't matter what was going on, that the bombs were raining down, but he had to learn his one hour every single day.

There were not many Jews in Birmingham, and it was hard to get kosher food. My father wouldn't drink the milk because it was not *chalav Yisrael.* There was also a problem with the bread, since England bought flour from the United States that contained milk powder for added nutrition. Although it was kosher, the milk powder was not *chalav Yisrael,* so Father decided he would not eat bread baked with that flour.

A young religious Jewish woman who lived in Birmingham was the solution to his problem. She was married to a foreigner who had been deported to Australia. In order to support herself, the woman cooked lunches for the young people who lived in her area. My father was one of her customers.

Mother Arrives in England

My mother, Feiga Malka Schorr, was born in Yasse, Romania, on July 30, 1907. Her father, Reb Avigdor Schorr, was a great-grandson of the Rebbe of Ruzhin, Rabbi Yisrael Friedman, founder of the Ruzhiner dynasty. Reb Avigdor was a stepson of the Shtefeneshter Rebbe, Rabbi Mordechai Friedman, who raised him as his own son. (The Shtefeneshter Rebbe had no children of his own.) My mother's mother was a Twersky, also a descendant of the Ruzhiner dynasty.

Mother, known by the pet name of Lali, had been invited to come to England to visit her brother-in-law Rabbi Shmuel Sperber, who had married her sister Miriam. She arrived the day after Miriam gave birth to her second child, Avigdor, in order to help her out. At the time they were living in London. It was the summer of 1937.

My mother's mother, Bluma Raizel, was a sick woman, widowed years earlier. She suffered from kidney stones and required surgery. My grandmother's older brother, the Trisker Rebbe, or Fetter Leibenu, as the family called him, managed to obtain a visa for his sister. And so my *bubby* also arrived on British soil from Romania in 1937, together with my mother's sister Pearl, or Polly as she was known. After the surgery, my grandmother went to live with the Trisker Rebbe in Stamford Hill, together with Polly and my mother. Luckily both of the sisters found work not long after.

Dark clouds were scurrying across the European skies, obstructing the light of the sun. A chill fell over the land. War was creeping upon them slowly but surely. There was no way to prevent its coming, just as there was no way to prevent the movement of the clouds across the heavens. And then one day it happened.

My mother remembers clearly the day the war broke out in England. They were listening to the radio, and Prime Minister Chamberlain announced in a very serious voice, "We are at war." Then the sirens started blaring. Bubby heard the announcement and promptly fainted. It was December 3, 1939.

At some point, in the midst of these turbulent times, my mother's sister Miriam, or Manetchka as she was called, thought of setting up a *shidduch* between her little sister Feiga Malka and their uncle's younger brother Mechele. The uncle was Reb Yisroel, who had married my mother's aunt, Suranu Twersky. The two met and before long were engaged to be married. When my father proposed to my mother, he told her that she should be prepared for a very difficult life, since he had not put aside one penny in savings. Nevertheless, she accepted his proposal.

My father was living and working in Birmingham at the time of his engagement. He looked for a home that would meet their needs. Birmingham was an area that was frequently bombed because of its industrial nature. People were moving out as quickly as they could and into the outlying rural areas. As a result, my father found a house with furnishings for a very cheap price, but the contract of sale required the signatures of both husband and wife.

He came to London with the contract in hand. It was a short time before the wedding, and officially he was not supposed to meet his *kallah*. But due to the pressing nature of the circumstances, my mother, accompanied by her mother, met her *chasan* at the train station. She signed the contract, and, after exchanging a few hurried words with his betrothed, my father left immediately for Birmingham and work. During wartime the young bride and groom did not have the luxury of spending even a little bit of leisure time together.

A Wedding during Wartime

The wedding took place in July 1940 in the home of Fetter Leibenu, the Trisker Rebbe, in Stamford Hill, London. My mother was thirty-three, and my father was thirty. It was difficult to get a minyan together since the bombs were raining down in London and people had been evacuated to the outlying villages. Fetter Leibenu officiated at the wedding ceremony.

My mother suffered from migraines, and it was no wonder with everything that was going on that she had a terrible headache at her wedding and couldn't eat anything at all. In truth, this was to her good fortune. There was no meat or chicken to be gotten for the wedding meal, but someone got hold of some old fish in lieu of better fare. The fish was bad, and all the guests came down with food poisoning. Mother was the only one who hadn't eaten, so she was saved that fate.

Not surprisingly, none of the guests stayed in town for *sheva berachos*, and a day or two after the wedding my parents left for Birmingham. As sick as he was from food poisoning, Father met with some government ministers during the week of *sheva berachos*. The gravity of his work would not permit delays.

Mother moved to Birmingham, but Polly continued to live with Bubby in London in the home of Fetter Leibenu.

Then Polly started working as a physicist and was away from home most of the day. This created a problem, since Bubby was sickly and could not be left alone. My mother decided that the simplest solution would be for Bubby and Polly to move to Birmingham, and Polly would travel to work from there.

Each morning my mother checked on Bubby to see how she was doing and then would usually accompany my father to the office in another section of town for a few hours, where she did the secretarial work. There were days when Bubby did not feel well, and my mother decided to stay home with her. Then my father would go alone to his small office. The place was so dilapidated that you could actually see through the cracks in the walls.

Mother would make Father something to drink before he left for work and then queue on line for food. She would bring back the meager rations and prepare him something to eat. He took the food with him to the office since he moved around during the day, traveling between factories in Birmingham, London, and other industrial areas.

My mother served in the official capacity of the company secretary and received a government salary. She did the writing and typing for the business and returned home by bus whenever she was finished. Then she'd wait up at night for her husband to come home. Often Father would come home very late, midnight or later. Sometimes, after arriving home, he would study his blueprints late into the night. Afterward he learned.

The bombings were so severe that eventually my parents' house was the only one standing. There was no longer a minyan since most Jews had fled to safer places. The heaviest bombings took place at night. This was a terrible situation for Bubby because she suffered from high blood pressure. Finally my parents decided that at night they would sleep outside the city in a small village about a half-hour away. Mother rented two rooms from a farmer, one for her and Father and another for Bubby and Polly.

The physical conditions they lived under were close to unbearable. They subsisted on a meager diet, and the lack of variety surely did not supply the necessary nutrients. There was also the wet climate (which my father never got used to, and he contracted pneumonia repeatedly), lack of sleep, tension from the bomblings, and the exhausting work at the factory. Under such conditions most people would do the minimum required of them; certainly they would not take upon themselves additional endeavors. But my father was not one to compromise. No matter what was happening in his life, he could not be induced to give up his self-imposed program of learning.

My mother would be terribly worried those nights she waited up for Father, shuddering while the bombs rained down all around. There were times he couldn't get home because the rail tracks were being bombed. She sat up, sometimes till three o'clock in the morning, in the intense darkness of the blackout. It was a lonely and frightening time. How happy she was when, occasionally, a little mouse would come out at night looking for food. It wasn't the best of company, but at least she wasn't completely alone!

During this period, my oldest sister, Avigayil Chaya Udel, was born. That day, Friday, my mother worked very hard getting ready for Shabbos since they were having guests. She had chopped the coals for the fireplace and performed other physically tasking chores. She finished her work and lay down for a short rest before ushering in the Shabbos when she went into labor. Luckily for her, Father was home and was able to drive her to the hospital. Bombs exploded all around them on the way, but thank God they arrived safely.

As they entered the hospital, Mother was met by a nurse who appeared to be about ninety years old. All young, able-bodied people were away at the front. The nurse said to my father, "Go home. You can come back in the morning. The first birth always takes longer. Surely nothing will happen until then."

My father followed her advice and left. The baby was born shortly after without even having a doctor in attendance. The date was November 13, 1942.

With all of the upheaval going on, it was no wonder that Avigayil cried a lot as a baby. My father would hold her at night and rock her, murmuring, "*Leib! Leib!* — Love! Love!"

Living with bombs exploding all around was part of life, but one never quite got used to it. Whenever my mother went to queue on line for food, she felt uneasy about leaving Bubby alone, never knowing when the next bomb would fall. She finally made the decision to take Bubby and Abby with her shopping rather than worry about them while she was away.

A gentile woman came to clean the house once a week, and my mother took her along to help with the shopping. On one of these shopping excursions the air-raid sirens began blaring. People ran off to the public shelters as fast as they could to save themselves. But it was impossible for my mother to run to the air-raid shelter with an old woman, a baby, and packages, and there was nowhere to hide.

"Quick, Abby, get down!" She not so gently pushed the child onto the ground and lay on top of her to protect her. The gentile woman lay on top of Bubby instead of running off to the bomb shelter to protect herself.

They trembled with fear, waiting for the moment of impact. The air vibrated intensely as the bomb exploded on the ground. The streets in the area were strewn with glass from broken windows, but they came out of that shopping trip safe and sound.

Living in Birmingham was difficult for other reasons. Although Shabbos was a day of rest, which my father so sorely needed, for him it entailed strenuous effort. Each Shabbos Father walked one and a half hours to the shul of Rabbi Rabinowitz from Ireland (no relation). On the way he would meet the chief rabbi of Birmingham waiting for a bus to go to shul. I wonder what passed through the minds of both men as they greeted each other with "Good Shabbos."

"One Can Never Be Hurt Doing a Mitzvah"

One of the positive outcomes of my father's work was that he was able to buy a car for next to nothing. People were not driving their cars during the war, and it was very difficult to sell them because there was no way to obtain gasoline. My father had no such limitations due to the nature of his work. Since he produced war munitions in various factories in numerous industrial areas, he was permitted to purchase as much gasoline as he needed in order to travel between production sites. In fact, he was issued permits to drive more than one vehicle, and at one point he even owned three cars.

The reason my father needed more than one car was purely technical. The roads were full of potholes from the bombings, and as a result cars were always breaking down. When that happened, it was extremely difficult to find a mechanic to repair the car, since most able-bodied men were serving in the armed forces. My father's work was considered so vital that the government allowed him this leniency, and in this way he would have a vehicle to drive in case the other one was out of commission. The young boys who worked at the gas stations were sure that my father was some royal foreigner (they had never seen an Englishman with a beard), since he had the government's sanction for the purchase of petrol!

However, this privilege was granted my father only when he drove the car for the war cause. Under no circumstances was he allowed to use the car and its precious load of fuel for his private use.

My father was first and foremost a deeply religious person. He always looked for opportunities to do a mitzvah and to earn merit in the eyes of Hashem. He did not feel that using the car to perform a mitzvah was wrong. He was not using it for selfish gain, but only for spiritual elevation. He felt that this was one of the ways Hashem had provided to enable him to earn spiritual merit.

One of the mitzvos Father particularly wanted to fulfill was that of being *sandak* at a bris milah. The *sandak* is given the honor of holding the baby as the *mohel* performs the circumcision. My father felt that in the merit of performing this special task, at a time when Eliyahu HaNavi is present, he would have special protection and success in life.

This mitzvah was so important to him that he actually placed an ad in the newspaper stating that he was willing to pay people for the privilege of serving as *sandak* at the bris of their child. Since people were desperate for some extra cash in those impoverished war years, every once in a while my father was called upon to serve in this capacity. He knew that if he were caught by the police driving a car for personal use he would surely be imprisoned. But his love of the mitzvah outweighed his fear of capture.

Once my father was called to attend a bris in an outlying town, far from the industrial area in which he worked. The father was a soldier in the British army, and he had been permitted to go on leave for several days. The couple had found a *mohel* to perform the bris, and they called upon my father to be *sandak*.

On the way back to work, Father reviewed in his mind exactly what he would say if he were intercepted by the police. The permits for the car and for the purchase of gasoline were in good order. His credentials were also in good order. He had all the necessary papers with him. The only problem he envisioned was if someone asked where he was coming from. The authorities would not believe he was traveling for his work since the area he was driving through housed no factories.

His appearance might also evoke suspicion. Englishmen were clean-shaven, even religious English Jews. During that time enemy spies were dropped by parachute onto British soil, and anyone who looked a bit unusual was suspect. As a result, my father was often stopped for questioning, and the young boys manning the gas stations had called the police many times when my father stopped for gas, certain he was a German spy.

On his way back from the bris Father found it necessary to stop for gas. As happened so often, he was taken to the nearest police station. He was questioned extensively, and many telephone calls were made to various government ministries to verify the authenticity of his credentials.

My father used this opportunity to help a friend of his. He told the police that although this man was a refugee his son had been serving in the British army for a number of years. Since he had no immigration status, the government officials wanted to send Father's friend to Australia. This would have been a calamity for the family. My father asked the police officials if they could intervene on behalf of this man. Even when he himself faced the possibility of imprisonment for infringement of the law, my father still kept in mind the plight of his friend.

Finally he was cleared by the presiding officer and was permitted to leave. The police had made countless calls and interrogated him thoroughly. Incredibly, the one question they hadn't asked him was "Where were you coming from?" Father always told us that one could never be hurt doing a mitzvah.

Mesiras nefesh, unusual commitment to do the will of Hashem, has wide-reaching effects. Perhaps as a result of my father's *mesiras nefesh,* his friend was never deported to Australia.

The War Orphans

Just before the war broke out in Britain, the government evacuated women with young children from the cities and relocated them to small towns. This continued throughout the war years.

My mother's sister, Miriam Sperber, and her family lived in one of these villages for a time. In 1939 Uncle Shmuel was hired as the religious educator of a group of 150 boys and girls who had been brought over from Europe. They were housed in a castle in Wales donated by Lord Dundonald for the purpose. Aunt Miriam served as housemother. They lived there until 1941, when the noble requested that the group vacate the castle. They relocated to various places in small groups.

One of the miracles of the war was that England allowed children's transports, or *Kindertransports*, as they were called, from mainland Europe into the country. As a humanitarian gesture, the English government allowed Jewish organizations, such as Bnai Brith, to rescue children from the claws of the Nazis. These children, of all ages and nationalities, came to British shores, leaving their parents behind, often never to see them again. They were placed with gentile families in the countryside.

Some of these children were raised lovingly by their adoptive families for many years and were lost to *Yiddishkeit*. But some left these homes after the war and were able to regain their Jewish identity.

Rabbi Dr. Avigdor Schoenfeld and Dr. Judith Grunfeld were instrumental in rescuing many of these children. Rabbi Schoenfeld put up a large number of girls in his mother's house in London, turning it into a home for them and providing them with a Jewish education. He visited them every Shabbos, and they looked upon him as their father. He also traveled all over Europe, bringing orphaned children to British shores and placing them with Jewish families. He called upon the Jews of London to respond with proper Jewish mercy and to adopt at least one Jewish child.

My mother and father discovered a Polish orphan, a very beautiful and intense girl named Perla,* living near Birmingham. My mother nicknamed her "the Jewish beauty." Father was driving home one day when he saw her at the bus stop. There was clearly a Jewish look about her, and he offered her a ride, which she accepted gladly. He discovered that she was, indeed, Jewish and living with a gentile family. He invited her for Shabbos, and she agreed to come. My father picked her up by car every *erev Shabbos*.

The first time she came Mother arranged for Perla and another girl to sleep in Father's study. When my mother showed her the room, Perla stood at the door and would not enter, staring fixedly at the rows of *sefarim* on the shelves.

"What's wrong?" Mother asked her. "Perhaps you don't want to share the room with this girl?"

"No, it's not that," Perla answered sadly. "This room looks just like my father's study at home. I can't go in there. How can I go in, alive, when I see him standing there with a *sefer* in his hand?"

My mother had no choice but to settle her in another room for the duration of her stay.

Later Perla showed my father her father's siddur, the only thing she had left of him. She told my parents that before he died her father told her when it would be halachically permitted for her to commit suicide. She came to them for Chanukah, and when my father lit the candles, she cried inconsolably. My parents wanted to help, but she rebuffed their displays of warmth and affection. She was torn between two worlds, the world of her past, which she found so terribly hard to give up, and the world of her present existence, which had a sense of unreality to it.

Perla continued to come for a number of Shabbosos, until my parents moved to London, shortly before Pesach.

During this time, Rabbi Rabinowitz, one of the Orthodox rabbis in Birmingham, was approached by a local priest.

"Rabbi Rabinowitz," he said, "I don't know if you are aware of it, but some of our good citizens living in the mining village of Chase Terrace have opened up their homes to your children. These good people have taken care of these unfortunate children as though they were their own and have come to love them dearly. They will be happy to continue caring for them and raising them as their own. I just thought that since they are Jewish, you may wish to take them back to your community. If not, we will continue to look after them just as we have until now." He provided Rabbi Rabinowitz with the addresses of the homes that were housing the children.

The rabbi saw that a transport of sixty-four Jewish children had been placed in gentile homes in Chase Terrace. He thanked the priest for the information and told him he would look into the matter. He was close to my father and immediately contacted him to discuss the situation. They were amazed at the honesty and sensitivity of the priest who had approached Rabbi Rabinowitz of his own volition. They formed a committee and, in my father's car, drove out to the mining village to find the children. They tracked them down and began devising a plan for bringing *Yiddishkeit* to them and bringing them to *Yiddishkeit.*

It would not be an easy job, getting the children away from their foster caretakers. Many of these families would not want to give them up. And possibly many of the children themselves, who could no longer remember their original homes, would not wish to leave their adoptive parents. But the priest had given the Jewish community the option of trying.

As far as the *Yiddishkeit* of the children was concerned, the situation in the village was pitiful. The Bnai Brith organization had sent only two boxes of matzos for all the boys in Chase Terrace for Pesach. A boy named Kurt, who had come from an Orthodox home, told my mother, "I ate *chametz* all of Pesach!" The children were learning that it was not the end of the world to eat *chametz* on Pesach. Tragically they were learning that one could live a life different from the way they were brought up at home.

Now started a new battle in my father's life. Before actually removing the children from their foster parents, he had to receive official permission to do so. He discovered that Bnai Brith, a Reform Jewish organization, had been responsible for arranging the children's transports out of Europe and placing the children with their foster families. My father was informed that he must obtain permission from Bnai Brith before making any changes in the children's living arrangements.

Unfortunately, these Jews were not connected to their spiritual roots. The philosophy they followed in this situation was that they were saving these helpless children in order to enable them to live a new life as upright British citizens. It made no difference to the Bnai Brith members whether or not the children continued living their lives as Jews. In fact, they were actually opposed to them remaining religious — they did not want these children reverting to the "ghetto Jew" mentality. In the midst of the bombings and war production deadlines, my father had to find the time and the strength to fight Bnai Brith.

Father was up against a fierce enemy. He discovered that the president of Bnai Brith was a noblewoman by the name of Dame Leslie.* He appeared in her office without making a prior appointment.

"What are you doing to these children?" he shot at her.

"What business is it of yours? We are taking care of them!" she retorted.

"I want the children!" my father insisted.

"We brought them here. They are our children to take care of!"

Father was adamant. "They are living with gentiles!"

"Do you want them to be killed by the bombings?" Dame Leslie inquired.

"These are Jewish children, and they are eating *treif* food. That is worse than dying!"

"It can't be helped." Dame Leslie was coldly dismissive.

But my father wasn't finished yet. "It can be helped. I will take the children and provide them with all of their needs."

"We are taking care of them and providing homes and an education for them. We don't want 'ghetto Jews' to settle in our country. Get out now!"

Father was forced to leave, but he kept returning, appealing to Dame Leslie in various ways. He showed her in writing that he was prepared to undertake completely the care of the children and all the financial responsibility. Likewise, she would be released from any and all responsibility to these children. All she had to do was sign the letter of release he had prepared for her with the committee members' signatures. The dame was not receptive to my father's offer. She consistently refused his request and turned him away time and again.

This did not deter my father from continuing his visits to her, relentlessly insisting that she allow the children to be removed from their gentile homes. Often, when Father reappeared in her office, she would shout excitedly, "Oh, I'm going to faint. I'm going to faint."

After a while the dame refused to have him admitted to her office. My father would not be put off. He forced his way in to see her, despite the fact that she always sent him away. Once, when he managed to get in, she became hysterical.

"Oh no, he's here again! He's here again!" she shouted. "The Queen will hear about this! I will call the police!"

"That's right," my father shouted back. "I want you to call the police. Then I will tell them exactly what you are doing. I want the Queen to hear about this, about the crime you are committing against these innocent Jewish children! Placing Jewish orphans with gentile families, not giving them the opportunity to grow up as their parents would have wanted them to. Yes, please let the Queen know so that I can publicize the atrocity that you are committing. I am going to publish this scandal in all of the newspapers!"

She promptly went into a swoon. "Oh, help me! Water! Water!"

A servant quickly ran over and splashed her face with water. "Look what you are doing to her!" he shouted.

Dame Leslie realized that Father would not leave her in peace, that he would push her into a corner until he broke her will. She was also afraid of the publicity. And so, out of desperation, she acquiesced to his request.

"Give me your paper to sign!"

She signed over full responsibility of the children to my father, including their financial upkeep. This was a major accomplishment, and I'm sure Father felt that he had fulfilled the mitzvah of *pidyon shevuyim,* redeeming captives, and of *matir asurim,* freeing prisoners.

All in all, twenty-five of the sixty-four Jewish boys, ages 12 to 16, were rescued. The committee of Jews from Birmingham established a hostel to house the boys and give them a Jewish education. My father advertised for a couple to act as housefather and mother. He found some wonderful people to fill the job, Rabbi and Rebbetzin Koehler from Germany. Rabbi Koehler provided the children with their spiritual needs, and Rebbetzin Koehler kept the hostel clean with the help of the boys and cooked for them. Father made sure that the hostel was well run for the duration of its existence.

At my father's *shivah,* I was privileged to meet some of these boys and hear their stories. This is what Gus Meyer told me:

"In 1938 we were in a hostel in Margate. We were sixty-four boys, mostly from Germany. In 1940 we were evacuated. The whole town of Margate, including the gentile children, were evacuated to the Midlands. The sixty-four boys were evacuated to a little mining village called Chase Terrace in Stradfordshire, and we lived with gentile families for two years.

"Rabbi Mechel Rabinowicz lived in Birmingham at that time, not very far away. He found out about us via the Bloomsbury House. That was the headquarters of an auxiliary in London that took care of refugee children. They were not concerned with religion. Their only consideration was that we survive. Rabbi Rabinowicz arranged for Mr. Benny Winter from Birmingham to come every Friday, leaving his family in London, and make Shabbos and *yom tov* for us.

Mr. Winter was our teacher and guidance counselor. We ate and davened together whenever Mr. Winter came. The villagers were very cooperative and gave us whatever we wanted. Although they cared for us, they believed we belonged with our own people.

"From the age of twelve until I was fourteen I lived with a family called Holt. Chase Terrace was a mining village, and very few of the local villagers were educated. But the Holts were educated people, and they were very good to me. They wanted to take care of me and send me to Oxford University. They said I was intelligent and could do well. They did it out of the goodness of their hearts. They didn't need the few pennies they got from the government for taking me in.

"None of us went to church because of Mr. Winter. That much of an influence he had upon us. But there was no future for us living among non-Jews. At the beginning I wouldn't eat meat. But then I started to. At first I always wore a yarmulke; then that went, too. I felt no pangs of conscience. We were so young, and we had no guidance. We were growing boys, and we craved food. If your father would not have come along when he did, we would have continued down that path, eventually assimilating with the goyim.

"Your father saw a need to organize a hostel where we could come back to *Yiddishkeit*. He had to fight Bloomsbury House, since they didn't care in the least about our living with non-Jews. After he got official permission to take us, your father went around to all the homes, asking the boys to leave their adoptive families and come with him. Of the sixty-four boys, only twenty-five came to live in the hostel in Aldridge in Stradfordshire. The others felt very comfortable living with their non-Jewish families and did not want to leave. They were being given opportunities for education, for making it in the world.

"We lived in the hostel with Rabbi Koehler, his wife, and his two daughters. Rabbi Koehler made sure that his girls didn't eat or drink any differently from the boys; there was no favoritism. He came from Frankfurt, Germany, and he was a real Yekke. We boys lined up every Friday night so he could bless us. He also set aside a small allowance fund for each boy. He was a wonderful man, creating a warm and caring atmosphere for us. Later he became the rabbi in the *chevrah kaddisha* in the Adas in North London.

"During the time we lived in the hostel, we went to non-Jewish schools, but we attended *shiurim* given by Rabbi Koehler every day. Once I lost six weeks' pocket money because I went with my head uncovered. I wasn't used to keeping it covered anymore, but he was very particular about things like that.

"Rabbi Koehler was Rabbi Rabinowicz's lieutenant. He received guidance and financial help from your father. Rabbi Rabinowicz arranged that we boys should go to a village near Birmingham for Pesach to be with *frum* families. He saw to it that we went to the dentist in Birmingham when we needed to, and he came to see that we were learning, that we were well clothed and well fed. He gave of his personal money as well as raising money for running the hostel. It is in his merit that we boys are who we are today."

My parents met Gus many years after they parted ways in England in a most unusual manner. In 1948 my parents moved to the United States and settled in Brooklyn. The heat of the summer months in the city was so oppressive that most families spent their vacations in the country, renting small wooden bungalows in small towns far from the city. In those days, many mothers were full-time housewives and did not work and therefore had the luxury of spending the entire summer out of the city. Fathers, of course, had to work during the summer months, perhaps taking off a week or two to spend with their families. It was common for mothers and children to live for several weeks in the country while fathers would come out only for weekends.

It happened one summer, when I was about twelve years old, that we were at Meislin's Bungalow Colony in a small town near Monsey, New York. One Friday night my father came running home from shul. He rushed into the bungalow, saying excitedly to my mother, "Do you know who I met here tonight?"

"No, of course I don't. Tell me."

"Gus Meyer, one of the boys from the hostel!"

"Do you mean it?" she exclaimed. "How absolutely wonderful!"

"Yes, he is staying in this bungalow colony. I didn't recognize him, but he recognized me the moment he saw me. He will come over to see us after the meal with his wife."

My father had not recognized Gus because he had been a boy of sixteen when they separated. Now he was a grownup, married and with a family. But my father hadn't changed much in the interim, and so naturally Gus was able to recognize him.

Later that night Gus brought his wife, Jeanette, over to meet our family. I remember the excitement of that encounter. It was truly a memorable event for all of them.

Gus remained a faithful friend of the family. The families would visit each other from time to time. My father attended the bar mitzvah of Gus's son Alan, and he was given a place of honor at the head table.

The Meyers made aliyah to Eretz Yisrael in 1970. They lived in Haifa for five years and then moved to Bayit Vegan in Jerusalem. Jeanette met my parents on the street one day. They were in Israel visiting my sister Chavi, who had hepatitis at the time. When my parents went back to the States, they lost contact with the Meyers for a while. Then, on another occasion, they met again in Bayit Vegan. My parents had bought an apartment there, and it was shortly before they were making aliyah. After that the two families kept in touch. It was amazing divine intervention that brought them together again as neighbors.

Gus had kept contact with some of the other boys, and he informed them of his amazing rediscovery of Rabbi Rabinowicz. There had been three brothers, the Freifelds. Reb Eliezer Freifeld became a big *masmid* in Gateshead and ended up learning there for eighteen years. Afterward he became a *rosh mesivta* in the *yeshivah gedolah* in Antwerp, Belgium.

Who can measure the wide-reaching effects of an act of *chesed*? As Chazal say, "One who saves a life is as though he has saved an entire world."

Living among Non-Jews

During the time that my parents lived in Birmingham they never ate meat, since my father was unable to verify the reliability of the local *shochet*. One day a Lithuanian Jew, a *shochet* by profession, turned up in town. He had escaped from mainland Europe and was passing through Birmingham. The local Orthodox *rav*, Rabbi Rabinowitz, knew the man personally and vouched for his credibility, assuring my father that he could rely on him completely.

Somehow my mother managed to buy a chicken and arranged for the *shochet* to slaughter it. She was in the house, holding Avigdor Sperber on her lap (the Sperber children lived with them for a while when their mother fell ill). Just then, the *shochet* walked in holding the dead chicken by its legs. Avigdor looked at the chicken in horror. From that day onward he refused to eat meat. Father and Mother, however, would have loved to be able to eat meat, but it was simply unavailable in Birmingham.

My parents celebrated their first Sukkos together in Birmingham. My father was so occupied with meeting his production deadlines that he did not have a free minute to think about building a sukkah. My mother found the solution to their problem. There was a small coal shed in the yard, completely black inside and out. She dragged over a ladder and unscrewed the roof. Then she whitewashed the walls. What would she do for *sechach*? My father worked long hours and came home late at night. She knew it would be up to her to find the solution or there would be no *sechach*.

Mother looked around the property for an idea and suddenly noticed the ivy growing up the side of the house. With great effort she managed to saw off a section of it. She dragged it over to the hut and managed to get it positioned atop the shed. It was a perfect fit.

The next year my parents celebrated Sukkos in the small village outside Birmingham where they slept at night. *Yom tov* was approaching, and again my father had no time to build a sukkah. He needed a carpenter, but all able-bodied men were in the army.

Father made inquiries until he met an old gentile who had spent most of his life working as a carpenter. He asked him to come over and showed him the veranda where he wished the sukkah to be built. He explained to him that he needed a three-walled construction to form a little hut.

"And what kind of roof do you want, a metal one or a wooden one?" the old man asked.

"Oh, that's all right. I don't need any roof at all," my father answered.

"What do you mean, you don't need a roof? Listen, sir, I'm an old man. Why are you making jests?"

My father ran into the house for a dictionary to look up how to say "sukkah" in English.

"It's a tabernacle!" Father said triumphantly when he came back out.

"A tabernacle? Oh, a tabernacle! Why didn't you tell me? It's going to be the Feast of Tabernacles!"

The old man was excited. Most likely he read the Bible every night and was familiar with the term. "I'll make you a lovely tabernacle, don't you worry."

My father had to rush off to work. When he came home that night, he inspected his tabernacle and realized that the man had knocked in nails to hold it together. The halachah states that certain materials, nails, for example, must not be used in the part of the sukkah that supports the *sechach*. He had forgotten to tell the carpenter to construct that part of the sukkah without nails. He would have to bring the old man back.

"Well," my father told the carpenter upon his return, "you certainly made me a very beautiful tabernacle, and I thank you for it."

"Glad you like it, sir. I always do my best to please."

"There's just one slight problem," Father continued. "Could you please pull out the nails holding up the cross beams?"

"Did I hear you right, sir? You want me to pull out the nails?"

"Yes, that's what I said."

"Those beams might come tumbling down in the rain and wind if they aren't nailed down," he countered.

"Have no worry. This is the way we always do it."

"Whatever you say, sir. Whatever you say!" the old man said, shaking his head in wonderment. He pulled out the nails until my father was satisfied that the sukkah filled all of the halachic requirements.

"That's wonderful. Just exactly right. How much do I owe you for the job?"

"Oh, I'll send you a bill."

The man left, and my father looked for something with which to decorate the sukkah. All he had was a painting they had once received as a gift. He banged some nails into the frame to attach it to the wall, and that was the extent of their sukkah decorations.

Sukkos came and went, and there was no bill from the old carpenter. My father didn't even know the man's name. He asked around and finally found out where he lived. He traveled to that little village after work, driving around in the pitch dark of the blackout in order to take care of his debt.

"Hello, there. I owe you money and came to pay. Why didn't you send me a bill?" Father asked the old man.

"It's all right, sir. You don't have to pay me anything. I feel it was a privilege to work for you."

"It's not all right. I must pay for the work I receive," my father answered him.

"Sir, you are making such a sacrifice for your religion. A man sits in the dark, in the rain and cold, without a roof for eight days, and I should take money for it? No, sir, no!"

"You are right, but I am also right. I can't take your services for nothing. I would feel as though I were stealing. I will give you the money, and you do with it as you wish. It is your money. You have earned it."

"Fine. In that case, I will give the money to my church."

My father was taken aback but answered respectfully, "It is your money. You can do with it as you like."

Once again, my father had created a great *kiddush Hashem.*

On another occasion my father had no *esrog* and *lulav* for Sukkos. It was impossible to find an *esrog* in England during the war. The Skolyer Rebbe was living in New York at the time, and he sent his brother an *esrog* and *lulav* by air mail. My father brought the package home from the post office and opened it up in eager anticipation. To his dismay he found that both the *esrog* and *lulav* were cut to pieces. The package had gone through a security check, and the authorities had made sure that there was no bomb inside. Regretfully the *esrog* and *lulav* were now rendered invalid.

After much detective work my father discovered that in one town in England the Jews there actually possessed two *esrogim.* This was near a resort town with a kosher hotel not far from Manchester. My father spoke to the Jews of that town and explained to them that since that they had two *esrogim,* and so many Jews did not have any at all, it was only fair that they hand over one of the *esrogim* for communal use.

One of the *esrogim* was duly given over to the hotel in the resort town. My father decided to spend *yom tov* there so that he could take advantage of the precious *esrog* and fulfill the mitzvah of *arba'ah minim*. Many people came from Manchester to *bentch esrog* and *lulav* on this community *esrog*. It was in my father's merit that they were able to do so.

Pesach posed even more problems. Where would my parents get food for the *chag*? The food ration allotted one egg a week per person. The village farmer they rented their room from was a nice and decent man. Before Pesach my mother approached him and said, "Farmer Brown,* you know our festival of Passover is coming up."

"Oh, right," he said. "We know all about that. Me and the wife study the Bible before we eat."

It was true. Each night they would wash up from their hard labor, dress up, and sit before the fire and study the Bible. Only then would they have their supper.

"How wonderful," Mother responded. "During the eight days of the holiday we must prepare festive meals on four of these days. I was wondering if we could have next week's egg ration this week?"

"Sorry, Mrs. Rabinowicz. I would love to help you out, but the government doesn't allow us to." My mother could see that he really felt badly about it. "But you know what? Me and the missus will give you our egg ration for this week. So you'll have the four eggs instead of the two for the week of Passover."

"Thank you so much, Farmer Brown!" my mother exclaimed. "That will make a big difference to us, and we appreciate it greatly!"

The Skolyer Rebbe sent them matzos from America, and

the Jewish families living in the nearby villages pooled their raisins and made grape juice. There was a meager amount for each family, less than the required four cups, but it was better than none at all.

On the day of *bedikas chametz* Mother and Father went to Birmingham to purchase whatever food they could find. They were still quite a distance from town when they had to stop because the roads were bombed out. The buses were stalled as well. For lack of any other option, they walked to Birmingham.

It was a long and tiring trek. To their dismay, they found the food market completely wrecked from a bomb. There was nothing to be bought. The only thing my mother found intact was some vegetable that resembled parsley.

"Look, Mechele, at these vegetable roots," she said. "I'll cook them in a soup."

"Good," my father replied. "At least we didn't come for nothing."

What could they do? This was the reality of war. They turned around and walked back to their car. It took them hours to return to the village. My mother took her precious vegetable roots to prepare the soup. Horror of horrors! She discovered that there was no water and no electricity! Many more hours passed until she was able to cook it. Since the Trisker Rebbe, Fetter Leibenu, was residing in the village at that time, my father decided to send Polly and Bubby to him, hoping they would have a more satisfying seder at the Rebbe's table.

The next night, exhausted from their trek of the day before, they ushered in seder night. My mother pulled up the couch to the table for my father to sit on, as for a king. She had no tablecloth for the table and used a pillow case instead. They had matzah, grape juice, an egg, the soup my mother had made, and their Haggadahs.

They began chanting the words of the Haggadah. Suddenly my mother opened her eyes. She called to my father, and he, too, opened his eyes. They looked around and realized that it was morning. They could not believe it. Had they really slept through the night?

"We're lucky we have two days to make a seder!" Mother exclaimed.

"Good thing I sent Bubby and Polly to Uncle," Father said. "I hope they had a normal seder there."

That was what it was like to live in war-torn Europe. That was what it was to live among gentiles, far from a Jewish community. Although the bombs were falling heavily in London, they were falling just as heavily in Birmingham. My parents made the decision to move back to London, to live among Jews.

Back to London

During the war years many people fled London, as my parents had. Houses went up for sale like weeds sprouting after a rain. But my parents wanted to live in a Jewish community, close to a shul, and therefore decided to move back to London.

Polly was working in Croiden, in the Port of London, at a chemical plant where explosive materials were produced for the war effort. She informed my parents that the Germans were now deploying a deadly new bomber, sending it over the English Channel from France. The V2 rocket was a pilotless plane that wreaked utter devastation wherever it hit. Polly warned my parents not to move back to London because of the danger.

But they had already made their decision. In 1943 they made the move with my sister Avigayil. My father bought a beautiful large old house, with all of its furnishings, for next to nothing in Cricklewood in the northwest section of London. They moved in on Rosh Chodesh Nissan, just in time for the Pesach holiday, and Bubby and Aunt Polly came to live with them once again.

Suddenly my father remembered Perla. He decided to make the trip out to the village in which she lived and bring her to London for Pesach. After a long and tiring drive, my father got to the house of Perla's adoptive gentile family and rang the bell.

"What do you want?" a man asked upon opening the door.

"I came to take Perla to us for the holiday," my father said.

"Her name is Maria, not Perla. No more visiting," he said. "She lives with us, and she's our child now."

My father saw Perla standing behind the man. He appealed to her with beseeching eyes.

"It's finished," she said to him with a deep sadness. "They take me to church." She turned away and disappeared into the depths of the house.

After that, hard as my parents tried to get Perla to come to them, they were unsuccessful. But although she refused to visit, she did write to them. Years later, when my parents were living in the United States, a letter of hers was delivered to Mother from Eretz Yisrael. Perla wrote that she had discovered that one of her relatives was living there and decided to join an illegal transport to Palestine. Upon making the trip safely and settling into her new home, she began a nursing course. She wrote that she finally felt settled and content.

It wasn't much after that when the War of Independence

broke out. The casualties were heavy, and many young people were killed. After that one letter from Eretz Yisrael, my mother never heard from Perla again.

The Ballroom

My mother often described that old London house with nostalgia. There was a big six-walled vestibule at the front of the house, richly paneled in wood, with a fireplace and large bay windows. On the lower level, there was a huge ballroom with a beautiful parquet floor and a little stage. My father had a mikveh built in the corner of the room since he had the custom of immersing in a mikveh daily before *shacharis*, the morning prayer. He learned *hilchos mikva'os*, which are very complex, to ensure the mikveh was halachically sound.

In all of Cricklewood there were only two *mikva'os*, the one in my father's house and one in the home of the Premishlaner Rebbe, Rabbi Margolies. There were community *mikva'os* for men and women in Golders Green, a different section of London, but during the war, with the bombs falling at night, it was nearly impossible to travel because of the blackout. So my father's mikveh served the local community, and they made good use of it.

The ballroom was also used for my father's *tzedakah* and community functions. He began a custom of having *melaveh malkahs* on *motza'ei Shabbos* for the local Jews. He served food and drinks, and they sang *motza'ei Shabbos zemiros* together. During the war people did not usually congregate in one area because of the bombings, but all the Cricklewood Jews came to my father's *melaveh malkahs*. He also invited local *rabbanim* to give Torah talks and other religious personalities.

Many of the Jews who attended this function were not familiar with halachah. The Cricklewood Jewish populace did not understand why the ladies could not sit together with the men. But they got used to the idea soon enough. It was wartime and food was rationed, yet my father managed to give the people a nice spread. It was worth it for them to sit separately from their wives in order to enjoy the food and the warm atmosphere.

Etel

The law in England during the war years was that women were required to serve in the armed forces or to do some other work for the war effort. Word had spread that if one was lucky enough to be employed in Mr. Rabinowicz's factory one would be exempted from army service. To this end, Etel, a simple Jewish woman from Carpartland, Russia, approached my father for employment.

The machine parts he produced had to be very precise in their measurements and therefore had to pass inspection before being shipped out. He hired several people, Etel included, to serve as inspection agents. In her hometown, the poverty was so extreme that children would begin working in the factories at six or seven years of age. As a result, she, a woman in her thirties, was totally uneducated in both secular and Jewish studies.

Then my father purchased the London house, and Mother now had a busy and full household. Etel changed her work locale. Father kept her on his factory payroll but now had her work in the house, helping my mother with the cooking and other chores. She knew almost nothing of *Yiddishkeit*, did not even know the *alef-beis*, and often stayed up late into the night asking Mother questions about the Jewish holidays and the various mitzvos.

Miraculous Protection

It was a most eerie sensation when the V2 rockets hit. There was no blaring of sirens to give advance warning of the attacks, since the rockets traveled faster than the speed of sound. One could hear the bombs exploding before hearing the jets flying overhead. Sometimes bombs fell very close to my parents' home, and the ceiling plaster would come raining down on them.

My mother was terribly concerned about Bubby's welfare in those frightening times, running to her in the dead of night to see how she was. It happened often that my mother had to grab Avigayil and her old, frail mother and literally carry them to the bomb shelter that had been constructed in the house. There was a room in the basement containing a heavy metal desk. Whenever there was warning of an impending attack, my mother would put Bubby and Avigayil underneath it.

Often my father had dreams of impending disaster. He always took his dreams seriously, and he would fast the next day. This is known as a *"ta'anis chalom,"* fasting as a result of something one has been told or seen in a dream. If the dream contains certain criteria, one is halachically required to fast, even on Shabbos.

It happened once that my father was fasting as a result of one of his dreams. This fast came almost on the tail end of a previous one. During the war, food was rationed and could be purchased only with food coupons. There was never enough food available to begin with. My father worked hard and was often weak from lack of sustenance.

"Please don't fast again," my mother begged him. "You never slow down your pace at work. How do you expect to have any strength?" Of course, he did not listen to her.

"What did you dream?" she wanted to know.

"I can't tell you," he said. "If you knew what the dream was, you too would want to fast. But let me say this. It is a *chesed,* an act of kindness from Hashem, that He allows us to fast. Believe me, it is worthwhile!"

That night was *bedikas chametz.* Father was still fasting. He was tired and went to bed early. In the middle of the night a bomb fell in the street parallel to theirs. There had been no warning sirens. The impact of the bomb was so great that the windows shattered, and the window frames fell out of the walls. Suddenly the house was filled with light.

During the war, a blackout was in effect in order to protect the populace from enemy bombers. All the windows were covered with black curtains to prevent light from the houses to be seen outside, cars drove without headlights at night, and the street lamps were unlit. Now, with all the windows knocked out of the walls, light from the surrounding houses escaped into the darkness of the night.

My mother jumped out of bed, grabbed the tiny Abby, and ran to Bubby's room at the other end of the house. She looked around and realized that my father was nowhere to be seen. She ran back to her bedroom and saw that my father's bed, positioned in the alcove under the bay window, was covered with the window frame and a sheet of broken glass. There was no movement under the covers, and she was sure that the worst had happened.

In shock, she carefully pulled at the bedcover. She managed to lift a corner of it and saw Father underneath. He was sleeping as peacefully as a baby, oblivious to all the mayhem. She called to him and he awoke. He climbed out of bed carefully, without sustaining even a scratch.

"You see that sometimes it is a *chesed* to fast," he told her. All she could do was nod in agreement.

The explosion was so massive that blocks of houses, perhaps thirty or forty homes, were destroyed. This was one of the most devastating bombings that had occurred in the area. The bomb had made a direct hit on a large house. Buried under that house were many people, including an old woman and her son on leave from the army. People from all around hurried to the scene to gawk at the devastation and to help dig out the victims from under the rubble. Men dug into the ruins to remove the bodies. It turned out that all the people, including the old woman and her son, were unharmed! No one even needed first aid since anyone injured had suffered only minor scratches.

Later on it was discovered that there had not been one fatality from this bombing. It was an outright miracle. My father was less incredulous than my mother. He knew that sometimes there is a need to fast when one receives a message via a dream. Hashem had sent advance notice of the tragedy and allowed one of His faithful servants to effect its outcome. My mother never questioned Father again about his fasts.

A Jew First

Upon his return to London, my father opened a small factory, similar to the one in Birmingham. He was employed by the government to check the precision of various instruments and to produce munitions. My father was paid a salary by the government and was not permitted to accrue any personal profits from his work.

As he had done in Birmingham, he hired as many *shomer Shabbos* Jews and refugees as he could. This was a godsend for many Shabbos-observant Jews; obtaining a job that did not require work on Shabbos in those times was next to impossible. The refugees he hired were saved the fate of being drafted or evicted from the country.

One Friday night, when my parents were sitting at the Shabbos table, a government official and two police officers came to their home.

"Where is Mr. Rabinowicz?" they demanded.

"I am Mr. Rabinowicz," my father answered.

"I am a government inspector," said the official. "I found that your factory is closed tonight. You must come with us."

My mother protested and begged them to wait until after Shabbos, to no avail.

"All right," Father said. "I will come with you now, but I must walk since I do not ride in a vehicle on the Sabbath."

They had no choice but to agree. He walked while they rode alongside him in their police car to the nearest police station, which was not very close by.

The officer in charge gazed at my father with a stern expression on his face. "Mr. Rabinowicz, are you aware that all war production plants are required to operate seven days a week, twenty-four hours a day, in three shifts, in order to ensure maximum efficiency of our war effort?"

My father responded calmly, "Certainly, sir, I am aware of this fact. But you see, sir, as an Orthodox Jew I am a Sabbath observer. We are commanded to rest on the Sabbath. It is impossible for me to have my factory in operation on the Sabbath."

"Mr. Rabinowicz," the man bellowed, "you are charged with the crime of having your factory closed on Saturday. Your crime falls under the category of jeopardizing the safety of our country during wartime, a most serious offense. We will inform you when the court-martial will take place. You are advised to hire the best lawyer you can find, and you may be accompanied only by your lawyer in court. Remember that failure to appear at the court-martial is a serious infringement of the law. You may return home now."

The police officer who accompanied my father home tried to explain to him the ramifications of his crime. He told my father that he need not bother to retain a lawyer, since the men in the tribunal that would try him were not judges by profession. They were army and naval officers, and in their eyes his offense was inexcusable. By jeopardizing the safety of the country, he would be found guilty of treason, which usually incurred the death sentence.

It was worse than that, my father thought to himself. He was not even a British citizen but was actually a former resident of Austria, an enemy ally. His travel permit classified him as "stateless," which implied that there was something suspicious about him. With his beard and quaint chassidic garb, he might even be seen as a spy in his accusers' eyes.

Father returned home to my frightened mother a few hours later and told her what had transpired. She became terribly upset.

"What's going to be?" she moaned. "What's going to be?"

"What is there to be afraid of? Hashem is with me!" he said in an attempt to calm her down.

Father decided to forgo the services of a lawyer (he didn't have the money for one anyway) and prepared his own defense. He spent the next few days and nights preparing the production records of the factory. He recorded all the orders he had received, when he had delivered the samples, and when he had filled the orders. His records were meticulous to the last detail.

The call finally came, informing him exactly when and where to appear in court. My mother was not permitted to accompany him, and she had an agonizing wait until he finally returned home at the end of the day. He announced simply that he was a free man and described the scene to her.

He had been led to a room containing a long table. There were many men sitting there, adorned with all sorts of medals. It was obvious that they were high-ranking army and naval officers. My father was asked where his lawyer was. He replied that he had prepared his own defense. Then he was asked to state his name, address, and occupation and to answer questions about the nature of his work.

He told them, "I have made a tremendous effort, working many extra hours, sometimes close to exhaustion, in order to meet my production deadlines. If you will examine the records I have brought of our production schedules, you will see that I have never missed my deadlines for government consignments by even one day."

They did a thorough examination of his records. One of the officers said, "Since you have been hired by the government as part of the war effort, and the law of the land is that any such enterprise must be in full production seven days a week, twenty-four hours a day, you are accused of jeopardizing the safety of our homeland, Great Britain. What do you have to say in your defense? Keep in mind that if you are found guilty you may incur the death penalty."

"I felt no fear as I looked into their eyes," Father told Mother. "I knew exactly what I was going to say. I told them, 'I may not operate my factory on Saturday. God does not permit me to work on the Sabbath.' "

"We also have a Sabbath — Sunday — but we go to work. We are in the midst of a war!" his accuser countered.

"I am prepared to go to jail for my religion," Father responded.

"Explain yourself. How can you jeopardize the safety of an entire country for the sake of the Sabbath?"

"My dear, honorable officers, I am a newcomer to this land of England. I have chosen to live in this country because you are the defenders of democracy. You are fighting the forces of evil in the world and saving the lives of the many innocent brothers and sisters I left behind in mainland Europe. I wish for victory for our homeland surely as much as you do.

"What I realize, however, is that this war that we are fighting is not a war like other wars. It is not a natural war. It is not two nations or a number of nations fighting each other. I see clearly here that in this war a group of allied nations is fighting a Satan. This devil has otherworldly powers. In order to be able to successfully overcome this Satan we must elicit the help of God in Heaven. He has the ability to destroy this inhuman man and to allow the forces of democracy to rule throughout the world. And so I pray daily to our Father in Heaven that He deliver the enemy into our hands, to stop the deaths of our noble and good English citizens, and to allow us to end the war.

"But, my dear gentlemen, in order for me to find favor in my Father's eyes, I must do His will. Why would He listen to me and answer my plea, why would He help me, if I disobey His word? I am a religious Jew, and our code of law is the holy Torah. One of the commandments of our Torah, as I am sure you are aware, is to honor the holy Sabbath. For us, this is the seventh day of the week, Saturday. If I were to transgress the holy Sabbath, not only would I not find favor in the eyes of God, but He would certainly pay no attention to my pleas of mercy to Him. And so, as part of my efforts toward winning the war, I am doing whatever is in my capabilities to win God's favor and to get Him to fight our battle for us. I am quite sure that without His help there is no way that we could possibly overcome this devil in human guise.

"And so, gentlemen, by keeping my factory closed on the holy Sabbath and fulfilling the will of God, I am actually helping you win the war. May God be with us and bring victory to our land."

The men were silent for a long moment as they absorbed my father's fiery words. Then they all stood up for him. They were visibly overcome with emotion, something the proud Englishman rarely exhibits. One by one they extended their hands to shake my father's. The death tribunal unanimously waived the charges against him.

My father's chief accuser said, "Continue working as you

have until now, continue observing your Sabbath, and continue praying for our victory!"

Each one of the judges wished my father well and excused himself for putting him through this frightening ordeal. He was led out of the courtroom with dignity and respect.

And so ended a very trying episode in my father's life. Once again, he created a tremendous *kiddush Hashem.*

There have been many other incidents during his work for the government that created a *kiddush Hashem.* My father was once given a blueprint for a very intricate and very costly piece of machinery. It may have been part of an army tank or even a plane, and he was commissioned to produce a large quantity of them.

He studied the blueprints carefully for two days and nights. Something was not right, and he could not figure out what it was. Finally he found the minuscule error in the plans. He spoke to the ministry involved and told them of the mistake he had found.

"Impossible, Mr. Rabinowicz," he was told. "These blueprints were designed by the most qualified engineers in the country."

"Well, then, sir, I cannot accept this order, since I am certain that the plans contain an error. I think it is in your best interest that you meet with me so that I can explain the mistake to you."

My father had a hard time getting them to agree to meet with him. But he persisted until they acquiesced.

It was a bitterly cold day by English standards, and the snow was falling thickly. My father had been told to appear in some out-of-the-way, high-security complex. Going there entailed a lot of time and effort for him, and he would reap absolutely no monetary gain from it. It was my father's integrity that made him go.

The complex was high-security, indeed, and he had to pass through some ten checkpoints before he got inside. He met with several highly placed engineering experts. My father was not in the least intimidated as he presented his criticism of their plans. It took them some time until they realized their error, but he proved his point.

They were flabbergasted. They could not get over their amazement at this young, uneducated foreigner with a mind so sharp that he could catch a tiny error that highly trained professionals had not caught. They were equally impressed by his dedication and perseverance. Although the government was saved millions of English pounds by his pointing out the error in the plans before production began, my father did not gain one extra pence for his efforts. He continued, as before, to earn a meager salary.

As a result of this incident, my father created a great revolution in various government ministries. He received many phone calls and letters from high-ranking government officials lauding him for the great thing he had done and for the tremendous amount of money he had saved the government. At the end of the war the Queen commended him for his dedication to the war effort, and he and his family was offered honorary British citizenship, something so rare that it was almost unheard of.

Others in my father's position embezzled millions of pounds during those years, acquiring personal fortunes at the government's expense. Father was content to earn whatever he was given and used his small income to serve Hashem faithfully. And one of the ways he served Hashem was by acts such as this, acts that created a *kiddush Hashem*.

Another amazing story also involved a huge sum of money. Father had filled a large order for the government and was sent payment for it. Upon checking the figures, he realized that he had been grossly overpaid. Immediately he called up the ministry that had given him the order and told them of their error. He let them know that they had credit with him and asked them to send him a letter of confirmation of their conversation.

He never received the letter. He called the ministry several times, and they said that they appreciated his honesty and would take care of the matter. Still no letter arrived. He then informed them that he wanted to return the extra money, but he wanted to be sure that the error would be adjusted in their bookkeeping records. He never heard from them, and no one came to his office to collect the money.

The temptation to keep the money was great, but my father felt deep down that this was the wrong thing to do. Finally he asked his brother-in-law Rav Shmuel Sperber for advice. Rav Sperber told him that according to halachah, if a Jew makes an error to his disadvantage, the recipient is required to return the extra money. If a gentile makes an error to his disadvantage, the recipient is not required to return the money. However, it is a praiseworthy thing to do since it creates a *kiddush Hashem*. My father decided once and for all to send the ministry a check in the amount he had been overpaid, with an accompanying letter. Once he did so, he immediately felt better about the whole business.

My father's letter and check were acknowledged. In a subsequent correspondence, he finally discovered what had been going on. It seemed that the accountant made an error when paying my father for the goods he sent them. He had mistakenly added several zeros to the figure on the check. When my father called to bring the error to the ministry's attention, the accountant was in a dilemma. He did not want to admit his incompetence. So he said nothing about it, and nothing was done. Until my father's check arrived, no one other than the accountant knew about the mistake.

In the letter they sent my father, the government officials praised him for his honesty. The sum of money he had returned was enormous; in today's figures it would have been worth close to a million dollars. In later years, when my father needed credit references in order to obtain a loan, he gave the bank the names of the people at the ministry involved in this incident. When the bank manager got back to Father, he told him that his credit status at the bank would be unlimited! He had heard such unbelievable praise of my father's integrity that he knew that no matter how much money the bank loaned him they need never worry about it being returned.

My father was recognized by the government ministers for his genius and dedication. He was often asked to come to one of their facilities and do some voluntary scientific work during the war years. Sometimes he was asked to appear on Shabbos. Father asked a *she'eilah* and was told that he could walk there and do whatever he was able to do as long as he didn't violate Shabbos. He would walk to the facility in his Shabbos *bekeshe*, with no shame and no excuses for who he was.

As my mother expressed it, "He did so much for his own spiritual development, so much for the Jewish community, but, most of all, his greatness was in the *kiddush Hashem* he created over and over again in the eyes of the goyim."

The End of the War

I was born on September 15, 1945, after "Victory in Europe" day but still before Japan had capitulated to the Allies. I made my appearance in this world on Shabbos. My father brought my mother to the hospital on Friday, accompanied by the Sperbers. This birth was quite different from Avigayil's. It dragged on and on, hour after hour. Since the end was still not in sight, my father decided he would go to shul. My mother was not alone; the Sperbers were with her. It was while my father was away davening that I finally made my appearance. The name they gave me, Bracha Perel, was a girl's version of my father's father's name, Boruch Pinchas.

The moment the war was over Rabbi Dr. Schoenfeld traveled to Auschwitz and throughout Europe looking for Jewish children. He brought them to London and settled them with different Jewish families. My parents took in two orphans from Poland, a sixteen-year-old twin girl and a twelve-year-old boy. The twin girls, Tosia (Toshe) and Mariana (Miriam), had suffered unbelievable cruelty at the hands of the infamous Dr. Mengele. They had been in the concentration camps from the ages of nine to fifteen. They barely remembered what it meant to live in a home with a family. Toshe came to live with us, and Miriam went to live with neighbors next door, the Klapfishes.

Toshe and Miriam didn't come to England immediately after the war. After leaving Auschwitz, they headed back to their hometown, Lodz, to see if any of their family had survived. Sadly, they found no relatives there to take them in, and so they rented a room with friends and began working. Some time later, through amazing *hashgachah pratis,* they were reunited with their older sister, Chanke, who had been sure they were dead and was no longer searching for them. Chanke, too, had settled in Lodz. But anti-Semitism was still rampant, and the Poles did not want the Jews to return to their land. One day Toshe was attacked by a Polish man. Chanke made her sisters leave Poland with Rabbi Schoenfeld, and she left for Palestine as soon as she was able to.

The twins were brought to England in March 1946. A few months later Toshe arrived at the home of my parents. She adjusted well to our family, especially since she herself had come from a religious chassidic home. My father's davening and *zemiros* at the Shabbos table reminded her of home. She felt a part of the family and thought of Abby and me as her sisters. She loved to take us for walks and play with us.

Toshe tried to adapt as best as she could. After having lived so many years in the camps, she no longer remembered what a home was. But whatever she did, good or not, my mother and father treated her as their own.

My mother was excited about the prospect of having a teenage daughter, but this was a new experience for her. If a problem cropped up, and she wasn't sure how to deal with it, she would discuss the situation with her sisters, Miriam and Polly. She was very concerned that things should be handled right.

When Toshe first came to my parents, she had only one dress. My mother took her shopping to the big department stores in the West End. Toshe was plump and not as tall as the British women, and my mother had a hard time finding something that fit her properly. She did not give up. She ran from shop to shop just to find a dress that would fit.

My mother wanted to know about Chanke and how she was doing. She wanted to know about Toshe's past. Toshe couldn't talk about it. It was too soon. And there was something else. After Toshe came to England, she spoke of her horrific experiences. People didn't believe her, and it made her angry. But then she thought about it. *How can they believe me when I don't believe myself what I have gone through?* So she stopped talking.

My father wanted to know about Toshe's past, too, but he was very careful in asking about it.

Once some photographs were taken of her. My parents brought two pictures to show her. Toshe wanted to save them money so she said that she would like to have a copy of just one of them, even though she liked them both. My father said, "But, Toshele, look, you're beautiful in both of them." And he ordered a copy of both pictures. That was his way.

When my father decided to move to America, it was difficult for him to leave Toshe behind. He had such a sense of responsibility toward her and was so strongly devoted to her.

My parents told her to take a commercial course to learn typing and other practical applications to prepare her for being on her own. She enrolled in the Spittle Square Public Commercial School. When my parents left for America, Toshe moved to the hostel and continued taking courses at that school.

Eventually Toshe moved to Israel. Chanke was there, and she told Toshe that she must come immediately. Officially Toshe couldn't leave from England because, although the State of Israel had been declared, the British did not recognize the statehood. So when she traveled to Switzerland for a vacation, she went to France and from there took a ship to Israel. Miriam came later, in 1950.

My parents kept in touch with Toshe, writing to her in Israel, asking how she was, how Chanke was, how they were getting on.

Toshe came to visit Father in the hospital, close to the end. He appreciated it so much, was so happy that she came. He said, "You shouldn't have made the effort. You shouldn't have come." But for Toshe it was like visiting her own father.

My parents also took in a twelve-year-old boy named Victor Zhitto. They made Victor's bar mitzvah in their house. He had grown up in a nonobservant home, and for him the transition to my parents' home was much harder than for Toshe.

Victor's mother was killed during the war, but his father survived by crossing the border into Russia. Although he was unable to escape the Iron Curtain after the war, once he tracked his son to my parents' home he began corresponding with him and my parents. He sent my mother money to buy all sorts of things for Victor, such as tennis outfits, that did not blend in with our lifestyle. My mother tried explaining to him the incongruity of what he wanted for his son since the society he now lived in had a different value system. But the man was not interested in having his child raised as a religious Jew, and he continued with his requests, probably in order to keep his son from integrating with his foster family.

When my parents emigrated to the United States, they arranged for Victor to live with one of his English friends. Although he had been very attached to my mother, after my parents moved to the States he never once wrote to them. Now that my parents were gone, his father had more influence over him. Eventually Victor's father managed to get to Sweden and had his son brought to him. He raised Victor as a nonreligious Jew. This caused great pain to my parents, but the circumstances were out of their control. They could not prevent a child from being reunited with his father.

My parents had wanted to adopt the children. But English law stated that in order for adoption to take place one had to deposit a huge sum of money in an account for the adoptee. My parents did not have the necessary funds to do so, so legal adoption was an impossibility.

During those postwar years in London, different orphaned girls spent Shabbos with my parents every week. There was one girl in particular, Mala, whom my parents became close to. She was about eighteen years old, and she stayed with them for a short while. One day my father said to her, "Mala, I'd like to take you for a ride in the car and show you my shop."

"All right, Mr. Rabinowicz. I'm coming."

After driving for a little while, my father said, "Mala, I took you in the car because I didn't want the other girls to hear. Mrs. Rabinowicz and I have come to care for you since you came to us. We would like to make you a part of our family, to adopt you."

Mala was taken aback. My father reminded her of her own father. But since she hadn't seen her father and mother die, she still could not admit to herself that they were gone. In her mind, perhaps they were still alive. And so she couldn't allow herself to be adopted.

After a lengthy pause, she said, "Mr. Rabinowicz, I like your family very much, and I am very flattered by your offer. But I must refuse it. I cannot live with other parents yet. It is too soon."

Years later her story, *Alone in the Forest*, was published by C.I.S. in the Holocaust Diaries series. A few years ago I read the book and discovered her account of being hosted by my parents and their offer to adopt her as one of their own. As I read the fascinating story, I wasn't quite sure if she was referring to my family or not. But the moment she mentioned the twins I knew she was. I found out her phone number and called her up. She remembered me instantly, and she was terribly excited that I had contacted her.

"Perele," she exclaimed, "I used to rock you in your crib!"

I gave her my mother's number in Jerusalem, and they reestablished contact. On one of my visits to Israel, I made a special trip to London to meet her and to discuss that awesome time in her life.

Besides the orphans who came to live with us in London, my parents took in the Sperber children. After the war Aunt Miriam was stricken with tuberculosis and left for Switzerland to recuperate in a sanitarium. Danny, the third Sperber child, lived in my parents' house for a year and a half. He was about six years old at the time. It could not have been easy for my parents, but they did it, as they did everything, with generosity and modesty.

Besides the addition of the Sperber children and Toshe and Victor Zhitto to their household, there were people coming and going all the time. My father was concerned for my mother's welfare and felt that it would be difficult for her to care for the house and the children all by herself, so he hired help for her.

There was an Indian woman, Miss Collin, who served as a nanny for myself and Abby. Avigdor Sperber remembers her as the "aristocratic Indian nurse who took salt in her coffee and patched me up when I had an accident." She was not Jewish, and so after Kiddush the wine was removed from the table, and then she would join the family for the Shabbos meal.

Once Rav Elya Lopian, *rosh yeshivah* of Eitz Chaim Yeshivah, was a guest of my parents for Shabbos. Miss Collin was eating with us as usual. Rav Lopian was very careful to use the word *Christians* in the conversation rather than the word *goyim*. He knew that gentiles regarded the word *goy* as something derogatory, and he was fearful of hurting Miss Collin's feelings.

The Northwest London Jewish Day School

My father was always involved in the concerns of the community. I imagine that he held many meetings in the ballroom for forming committees and rescue commissions for the varied needs of the Jewish community. After the war, he realized that there was no Jewish schooling where they lived in northwest London. The Sperber children were attending non-Jewish schools. Our Avigayil was old enough for kindergarten, and Victor Zhitto was also of school age. Toshe was older, so she was able to attend Rabbi Schoenfeld's school in Stamford Hill. Due to the pressing need, my father decided to found a Jewish school in Cricklewood.

Establishing a religious Jewish school was no simple matter. There were a number of rabbis in London who were opposed to the idea. Their philosophy was the same as that of the Bnai Brith. They wanted the refugee children to live as upright English citizens, integrating with their host country as much as possible.

Despite the opposition, my father characteristically plunged into the task with great zeal. He turned first to the Premishlaner Rav, Rabbi Margolies. The *rav* was a close friend of the family, and he loved the Rabinowicz children dearly. On Simchas Torah he would take Abby on his shoulders and dance with her. My father davened in the *rav*'s shul during the week and holidays, and on the *Yamim Nora'im* he was the *sheliach tzibbur* for *shacharis*. The Rebbe said he would never miss the minyan in which my father was davening, since he loved it so. The Premishlaner Rebbe became Father's eager ally in his new endeavor.

Father formed a committee, found a building, and began hiring teachers. In his struggle to establish the school, my father insisted on making Rav Yechezkel Abramsky part of the school board.

Rav Abramsky was a newcomer from Germany and a very strong personality, fighting courageously to improve the situation of the religious Jew. Although he was the greatest *talmid chacham* in England at the time, he was not very popular; he was too religious for the average Englishman. One of his first major confrontations upon his arrival in England was in the field of kashrus. It was common knowledge that non-kosher meat was being sold with kosher meat labels. Try as they could, many *rabbanim* had been unable to stop the fraudulent business. When Rav Abramsky took the matter in hand, his unyielding efforts produced results. He was a force not to be dealt with lightly.

When the local rabbis, who were *dayanim*, and another rabbi heard that my father was involving Rav Abramsky in his plans for creating the new Jewish school, they became enraged. They wanted the school to be similar to the typical English school. Jewish education at that time consisted of Sunday school for several hours. Every big shul had a Sunday school. The only truly traditional Jewish school was Rabbi Schoenfeld's school for girls in Stamford Hill. Perhaps there were some small boys' schools that did not offer secular education as part of the school curriculum, but in general it was unheard of at that time to send Jewish children to a Jewish school full-time.

The rabbis were so furious that once, though my father was sick with the flu and bedridden with high fever, the three of them invaded his bedroom to take him to task.

"Mr. Rabinowicz!" they shouted. "What do you think you are doing? Why are you mixing into things you know nothing about? We are the leaders of the Jewish community here. We know what is good and proper for our children and what is not. Do you want them to go back to the old ghetto mentality? Do you want to create another Jewish problem?

And how could you involve Rabbi Abramsky with the education of our children? Our children will be brought up as good, upright British citizens, integrating easily into the lifestyle of the society."

My father had faced more formidable foes than they. He told them he was ill and asked them to leave. He was not willing to discuss the matter with them at the moment. They left him, and from that day he simply ignored them.

Eventually the Northwest London Jewish Day School came into being, with Rabbi Dr. Sam Kahn as principal. Once the new Jewish school got under way, Abby proudly entered kindergarten. My mother told me that when Abby went off to school I would feel lonely and wait for her return, looking out the big picture window for long periods of time. When I caught sight of Abby coming home from school, I would call out gleefully, "Here comes our little Abby! Here comes our little Abby!"

Victor Zhitto began school there as well, and the two Sperber boys transferred from public school to the new one. Years later Toshe made a special visit to the school on one of her trips to Europe. She reported back to my mother that not only is the school still in existence, encompassing both primary and secondary schools, but it is considered by the government to be one of the better private schools in England.

Father Is Recognized by the Queen

Now that the war was over, Queen Elizabeth wished to honor those who had displayed outstanding effort and unusual courage during the war. My father received an invitation to a banquet to be given by the Queen herself at Buckingham Palace.

My father called a lawyer friend of his. "Hello, John," he said, "maybe you can help me. I need some information."

"Sure, Michael. What's it all about?"

"I just received an invitation from Queen Elizabeth. She is making a banquet in Buckingham Palace to honor those who demonstrated outstanding effort and courage during the war. I was chosen to participate as a result of my work in producing war munitions. Tell me, John, what do I have to do when I come in the presence of the Queen?"

"You don't say! Why, that's beautiful! Wish I could be there with you. Let me look up the protocol, and I'll get back to you."

John called back not long after. "It's like this, Michael. You approach her slowly, reverently. When you get close enough, you go down on one knee before her and kiss her hand. There is no way out of it, Michael. That's the way it's done."

My father was relieved. "Thank you for the information, John. I guess this time I will have to forgo the honor."

My father wrote a beautiful letter to the Queen, telling her how proud and happy he was to have been chosen for this great honor. Then he graciously declined the invitation to the Royal Palace by fabricating a tale of illness. For years my mother kept the royal invitation to the banquet as a memento of their years in England. Unfortunately, during one of their many moves, it got lost.

Although he did not attend the banquet, he was still awarded honorary citizenship. On January 7, 1948, My father and mother became naturalized British citizens, and they received an official certificate of naturalization. (My siblings and I did not need to undergo naturalization, since we were British citizens by virtue of the fact that we were born there.) Years later this honor would be instrumental for my father in obtaining U.S. citizenship for himself and the family.

Father Is Not Easily Forgotten

After the conclusion of the war my father no longer had anything to do with the various government ministers that he had been in such close contact with during the war. One day my father received a call from one of these government ministers.

"Hello, Mr. Rabinowicz. James Halloway here. How are you?"

"Just fine, sir. And how are you doing?"

"Well, you see, I have something I would like to discuss with you. Would I be able to come over?" The minister sounded upset.

"Of course, of course." My father set up a time for them to meet. He was baffled. What could the man possibly want?

The day of the meeting arrived. My father noticed the strained look on the minister's face. Mr. Halloway was upset, and he got to the point fairly quickly.

"Mr. Rabinowicz," he said, "something terrible is happening in my family. I need to talk about this to someone. I am a respected man in my community, born and bred in England. I have been living for many years at my present place of residence, and I am blessed with many friends, associates, and relatives. Yet as I was thinking about whom I could discuss my problem with, I felt uncomfortable opening up to any of them. And then I remembered you. During the time that I knew you, you had impressed me as a very wise and compassionate person."

"I will be very happy to help you if I can," my father said.

"You see, it's like this. Something has happened recently that has created a dilemma both for my wife and I and for our children." He explained the problem and then said, "We thought perhaps of moving somewhere where no one knows us. But we have been living in our present residence for many years and have built up strong relationships during that time. I have been given important assignments in my ministry. Moving away would be a difficult step for us to take right now. I thought perhaps you might advise me as to the best thing to do."

My father was thoughtful for a moment.

"I really feel for you, Mr. Halloway. I sorely wish I could help you in some way. But what can I say? I hardly know you or your wife, what you want and aspire for in life, what your children need in life. This is a complicated issue involving many factors. Don't you have a priest you confide in and ask advice from?"

"Our priest has not been much of a help to me in years past, so I didn't even approach him with this problem," Mr. Halloway replied.

"All I can say, Mr. Halloway, is that you should pray to God that He give you the insight you need to continue your life together in the best way possible. I, too, will pray for your welfare." My father was sincerely touched by the man's plight.

"Thank you, Mr. Rabinowicz, for your time." Mr.

Halloway got up to leave and shook my father's hand warmly. "You helped lighten my burden just by listening. God should allow you to be a listening ear for many distressed people in the future."

They parted, and my father did not hear from Mr. Halloway again. After some months he heard that Halloway and his family had moved to Australia. Out of all the people he knew and interacted with during his lifetime, Mr. Halloway found none other than my father to confide in and spill out his woes to!

An End and a Beginning

When the war came to an end, so did the business. Quick Supply was closed down, and my father found himself penniless. The law was such that those who had earned a fixed income before the war were permitted to earn the same amount as government employees. However, the law stipulated, one could not profit from the war. Since my father had started earning money as a government employee only during the war, he was given the minimum wage. Now this meager salary was terminated.

Not only that, the government owed him quite a bit of money, as it did to many others. There were government orders my father had filled for which he had laid out money, and he had still not been reimbursed by the government. My father had commissioned other factories to produce armaments, and he had paid the factory charges himself. This outlay of money had entailed a great expense for my father.

In the postwar economic crisis, the British government could not pay its outstanding bills. It issued government notes in lieu of payment, redeemable ten or twenty years hence. My father had never taken an illegal pence for himself, although there had been plenty of opportunity to do so during the war. There were no savings from before the war. He was out of a job and, in those impoverished times, could find no means of employment, and he had no money to start a new business.

People were dependent on my father for their sustenance, and he felt a tremendous feeling of responsibility to all of them. But what could he do? It was a very difficult period in his life.

Despite it all, my father became transformed on Shabbos. When Shabbos came, he was completely oblivious to all of his problems, the financial problems, the responsibility to others. On Shabbos, dressed in his *bekeshe,* he became a different person, a Shabbos Yid. He had a tremendous ability to control himself and to transform himself into the world of spirituality. He had a real feeling for what Shabbos was, the same way he had the ability to block out everything and learn a *blatt* Gemara for an hour every day even with the bombs raining down all around him.

In order to earn a bit of money, my father started marketing his radio invention. He had to make samples and send them out and wait for someone to buy them. It would be a long time before he would make a return on his investment.

My father did not have much success selling his radio. Perhaps it was too expensive to produce. He felt he had no choice but to move on and look elsewhere for an income. That's when he decided to go to the "golden land" of plenty, the United States.

At that time, my father's oldest brother, Reb Dovid

Yitzchok Isaac, the Skolyer Rebbe, lived in Williamsburg in Brooklyn. He had arrived on American shores before the outbreak of the war. My father's other brother, Reb Yisroel, the Kishinever Rebbe, arrived in the United States in July of 1948. And, one by one, all of his sisters made it to the States, each with her own story of miraculous survival.

My father applied for and got a nonimmigrant visa to the United States. The travel document he obtained in London in June 1946 from the American consular service declared him to be "stateless." He obtained entry to the United States for two months for the purpose of conducting business on behalf of Quick Supply, Ltd. He extended his visa several times.

Father arrived alone on U.S. shores with the task of finding a way to support a wife and children. If he could obtain a visa for them, he would bring over the two foster children as well. He did not have an easy time of it, but he never gave in to despair. His iron will and trust in Hashem kept him going. He searched out ways of earning an income, struggling on his own for over two years, visiting home occasionally. During that time, on January 12, 1948, Boruch Pinchas was born.

My father was very homesick for his family. Finally he could take the loneliness no longer. One day he telephoned my mother.

"Malkale, how are you and the children?" he asked her.

"Good, *baruch Hashem*, good. How are you?"

"*Baruch Hashem*, fine, but I am very lonely for you all. I want you to come here with the children."

"Come to America? Leave England? Leave Mamenu? Leave Toshe and Victor? How can I do that?" My mother knew she would never get a visa for her frail mother and for the foster children.

"We will work on getting visas for all of them after we settle here. Once I have an income and a house, we will bring them all over," my father assured her.

"But how will they manage without me?"

"Don't worry, Malkale. We are not alone. Hashem is always with us. But I feel it is not good for me to be here without my family. I want you to come."

My mother understood how difficult it must be for him and resigned herself to the move. She desperately wanted to take her old mother with her to her new home, but Bubby was a very sick woman, and it was impossible to obtain the required visa for her. Heartbroken, my mother left Bubby behind with Polly. I do not remember my grandmother at all; I was less than three years old when we moved to America.

My father came back to England to sell the house and conclude any business he had there. My parents said farewell to this land that had served as their home for over ten years. The time had come to move on.

The United States

My father and mother stepped off the ship with their three children. They were now starting a new phase in their life. War-torn Europe was behind them. What would their life be like here in the "land of plenty"? My father was overjoyed to be reunited with his young family. He was confident that he would make it in their new home.

One of the first mitzvos my father wanted to fulfill once they arrived was to visit an aunt, his father's sister, Mime Bracha Zaltzman. His father's father, the holy Reb Eliezer Chaim, came from Yampela, Russia, with his daughter, Bracha, and his sons, Shmuel Avrohom and Boruch Pinchas, to the United States in 1887 to escape the persecutions of the chassidic Rebbes. During that time many other Rebbes from Russia escaped to the U.S. for this reason.

Several years later Reb Eliezer Chaim returned to Europe

with Reb Boruch Pinchas, leaving behind his other children. The Rebbe did not return to Yampela but wandered from place to place. When he finally decided to leave Europe, he embarked on a trip to Eretz Yisrael, but his daughter Bracha begged him to come back to the U.S. first.

The Rebbe returned to the United States in 1915 from Lemberg, Poland, and became ill not long after. He spent the last year of his life in America and never fulfilled his dream of going to Eretz Yisrael. He passed away on Iyar 5776 (1916). His grave has turned into a site for Jews praying for *yeshuos*, not only on his *yahrtzeit* but all year long.

Mime Bracha was an old woman now and was living with her children. My mother was enjoying the visit with the aristocratic old woman and her daughters, Francis and Hatti, when she noticed that I was nowhere in sight.

"Where is Perele?" she asked in alarm, and she went from room to room looking for me.

"Look at that!" she said to her cousins when she discovered where I had disappeared to. Old Mime Bracha was sitting in her tall-backed chair. I had found a little footstool and had pulled it up to her. I was sitting on it and resting my head in her lap. Mime Bracha was smiling in contentment at the little one who found her so comforting.

"She must surely think Mime Bracha is her *bubby,*" My mother explained to Francis. "My mother lived with us in London, and Perele was very attached to her. She probably doesn't understand the sudden separation from her grandmother. She has discovered a substitute *bubby.*"

My oldest daughter, Bluma Raizel, is named after my *bubby,* whom I was so attached to but do not remember.

Immigrants in the New World

My mother came to the United States with a tourist visa for herself and the three children. When the tourist visa expired, they got an extension. When that one expired, they got another extension. Finally they were refused any more extensions and were told by the officials that they must leave the country. By that time my sister Eva (Chava Gittel) had been born. She was a U.S. citizen by virtue of the fact that she was born there.

"Are you aware," my parents said to the immigration official, "that one of our children is a U.S. citizen? If our baby is allowed to stay here, then we should be permitted to stay with her!"

The official answered, "No problem, folks. Leave your United States citizen here with us, but you must leave."

My parents took us to Canada to try to obtain immigration status. After talking with a number of immigration officials and trying one idea after another, my father finally said in exasperation, "You know, in England, I did not have to request citizenship. The government offered me honorary citizenship."

He showed them the naturalization documents.

"Why didn't you tell us that? If you were offered British citizenship, then you must be a very special person indeed!"

Everyone knew that British citizenship was granted to foreigners only under very unique circumstances. It was considered a most unusual achievement.

And so my parents obtained their immigration visas. That was in December of 1953. In those days it was impossible to maintain dual citizenship. You were either a British citizen or a United States citizen. It was difficult for my father to give up his coveted British citizenship, and he kept it for another few years. As late as May of 1958 my father filled out an application to register his intention to retain citizenship of the United Kingdom. It was only on February 2, 1960, that we finally became U.S. citizens. I was fourteen years old. My father warned us that we must not swear our allegiance to our new country, but we could affirm it. And that is what we did.

Beginning a New Life

My parents settled in the Bay Parkway section of Brooklyn. They rented an apartment in the home of a dentist. Often I would go down and watch while he worked on his patients. Sometimes, when Dr. Gross had a frightened child for a patient, he would call me over.

"Come here, Pearlie. Come and please sit in my dentist chair."

I acted brave as I climbed into the big, scary-looking chair.

Dr. Gross would address his frightened young patient. "Look here. You see what I am doing? I'm taking the mirror and looking at Pearlie's teeth," and he would proceed to examine my mouth. Although I was quite young at the time, I had seen Dr. Gross do this so often that it was familiar by now and I had no fear of the procedures. Nevertheless, I did feel a bit apprehensive as I climbed into the big chair with the scary-looking instruments. The dentist would point out to the child how harmless it all was, and soon she would calm down. I came out of it feeling like a big hero, and Dr. Gross came out of it with a patient he was able to work on.

When I think back upon this incident, it strikes me that in some small way I was copying my father. He could not allow a situation to be so overwhelming to him that he could not cope with it. He knew that he could always do what he had to do. This was a part of his makeup, and he acquired it through his deep belief that Hashem was his constant companion.

My mother registered Abby, who was almost six years old, into first grade in a local public school. It was a mostly non-Jewish area, and she had no idea that there was a Jewish school nearby.

Abigail did very well in school and the teachers loved her. But one day my mother was walking in a different section of town, and she heard the voices of Jewish children davening. She looked through the window and saw a schoolroom. She made inquiries and found out that this was an Orthodox Sefardic Jewish school. Although we were not Sefardim, my mother so much wanted to see Abby in a Jewish school that she immediately transferred her there, to the disappointment of her gentile teachers.

A New Livelihood

My father struggled to earn a few dollars for us to live on. He could not earn a salary because in those days in was very difficult to find employment that did not involve desecrating Shabbos. He had no choice but to be independent. There were not many options available to him, and he did whatever it took to be self-sufficient. Sometimes the work was menial and involved spending time with people he would normally never associate with. This was a difficult time in his life, until he was able to establish himself as a respectable businessman.

At one point he hired a truck and driver and drove around looking for scrap metal. My father spent long hours in the truck, paying the driver by the hour. At the end of the day, they would haul their finds to a scrap-metal station, where the truck would be weighed with its contents. He was paid by the pound for the scrap metal. It was common knowledge that the truck weighers would cheat, and often they would pay my father less than his due. Sometimes he would earn such a meager amount that it did not even cover the rent of the truck and wages for his driver.

In the 1950s, America was embroiled in the Korean War, and aluminum was in high demand. My father began focusing on salvaging aluminum. He spoke to a Jew who worked in the business and told him his plan. He would bring the scrap metal to a smelting plant and have the junk metal smelted and the aluminum separated out. The blocks of aluminum could be sold for good money. My father explained to the man that he had no money to establish the business, but he was able to oversee it. What he needed was someone with capital to invest in the enterprise.

"Mr. Rabinowicz, it sounds like a good business, but how can I trust you with my money?" the man wanted to know. "I really don't know you."

My father showed him letters from England from the big firms he had dealt with. They had written highly of him in relation to his business dealings with them.

The man said, "Why didn't you show me these right away? After reading letters like this, I'm only too happy to give you the money for this enterprise."

The plant was in New Jersey. The laborers, mostly blacks, had to be highly experienced, since the work was fatiguing and dangerous. Many accidents occurred at the smelting plants. Once a laborer was badly hurt from the molten metal. My father went to his home to see if his wife was managing while her husband was convalescing.

After the Korean War there was no more demand for aluminum, and my father discontinued the enterprise. Happily he got out of that business fairly quickly.

Eventually Father opened up his own plant in Newark, New Jersey, Victory Small Arms, Corp., producing screw machine products, doing casting, forging, stamping, drilling, and welding. The victory over Hitler was still fresh in his mind, and that is most likely what led him to choose that name for his new business.

Moving to Boro Park

My father managed to save enough money to buy a house in Boro Park, which had a sizeable Jewish population. Abby and I were enrolled in the Beth Jacob School for girls, and Boruch went to Yeshivas Toras Emes. There were plenty of kosher groceries and bakeries. There were even kosher restaurants, and every once in a rare while my father would take us to eat out. We did it seldom enough that it remained a really special treat.

For himself, my father never wanted treats of that sort. He was very particular when it came to kashrus and did not want to rely on butchers who slaughtered thousands of fowls at a time. He ordered chicken only from a butcher who had a small enterprise. He knew that when this butcher salted his chickens he did the job more carefully than most butchers. Likewise, for many years we ate only calf meat at home. The ritual slaughter of beef on a mass scale was done in ways that could create halachic problems, and he did not want to rely on the *mashgichim*. Calves were slaughtered on a smaller scale, and the procedure was much easier than that of full-sized animals, which naturally entailed many more *she'eilos*.

The house in Boro Park, no longer standing today, is etched in my memory. I lived there until I married and moved away in 1965. I have many warm and happy memories of those years. We used to spend a lot of time as children playing ball on the front stoop.

At the beginning, we lived on the first floor, and the second and third floors were rented out. At some point my parents needed more space, and they took over the second floor as well.

Yoel and Rechy Weiss were our tenants there for three and a half years. Sometimes Yoel would come home loaded down with packages. When my father offered to help him carry the bags into the house, Yoel refused, saying he needed the exercise. Father countered by insisting he wasn't so old (he was about sixty years old at the time) that he couldn't help others, and he carried the bags into the house.

Another of our tenants was our cousin Reb Shmelke Leifer, Mime Perele's son, and his wife. They lived on the second floor for a number of years. My cousin told me, "I lived there during the time your sister Chava Gittel got married. Usually the day of a wedding everyone is very busy. But at three o'clock in the afternoon I heard your father learning Gemara in a loud voice. He must have sat there for at least an hour. The day he married off his child, when everyone has things to do, he was sitting and learning Gemara! For me it was an unbelievable revelation. I will never forget it."

The Queen Elizabeth and the Queen Mary

In the summer of 1954 my parents decided that we were all going to England to visit the Sperbers (Bubby was no longer alive). My father booked passage on the *Queen Elizabeth* luxury liner to take us to England and on the *Queen Mary* for the trip back. They were still being used for passenger travel in those days. (Later, when it was no longer profitable to use them as passenger liners, they were converted into floating museums.)

We booked passage in the cheapest section of the ship, at the bottom of the hold under sea level. Since these were the cheapest bookings possible, we did not get rooms near each other. My mother, Abby, Eva, and I were on one side of the ship, and my father and Boruch had a room on the other side.

The ship was as big as a large hotel; it even had an elevator. There was a movie theater and swimming pools, a church and a synagogue, a playroom with babysitting where parents left their children, numerous restaurants, game rooms, a regular dining room, and a kosher dining room.

My father decided to take us on a tour of the ship. We took the elevator to one of the higher floors, where the first-class rooms were located. Walking through the halls lined in thick plush carpets, we admired the paintings and crystal chandeliers. If not for the motion of the ship, we would not have been able to distinguish these hallways from those of a fancy hotel.

My father noticed that one of the rooms was unoccupied. We walked in, awed at the richness of the suite. The sitting room, with its well-stuffed couches and armchairs, led to a richly furnished bedroom. We looked around, wide-eyed; we had never been in a fancy hotel before. My father ushered us out of the suite rather quickly, fearing we might sample the comfortable-looking armchairs.

A few minutes later we found a restaurant. My father hoisted us up on the stools near the bar and allowed us to nibble the fresh peanuts that were put out for the customers while he studied the menu. He ordered freshly squeezed orange juice for each of us. How excited we were to be drinking this expensive orange juice in this exclusive-looking restaurant. To us it tasted better than the fanciest ice cream soda.

We returned to our cabins filled with excitement. I don't think my mother could make heads or tails of what we were saying as we kept interrupting each other's reports of our adventure.

The entire overseas trip took five days, and we were never bored. There was so much to do. The babysitting room was full of toys and games, and even just sitting out on the deck and looking at the ocean was fun.

As luck would have it, a storm hit, and we became ill, unable to keep any food down. I recall going to sleep in my bunk at night and finding myself on the floor in the morning. I yelled at Abby for pushing me off my bed, but she only laughed.

It was amazing to us that the stewards who came to clean our room acted as though nothing was going on. They explained to us that they had become used to the rocking of the ship, and it didn't affect them anymore.

When we finally felt well enough to go to the dining room to eat, my father held my hand tightly. Although the storm was over, the sea was still agitated, and it took quite a bit of effort to walk without falling.

We spent a summer filled with fun with our cousins in London and returned back home in the month of September. We came back on a different ocean liner, and, as usual, I made friends with everyone, including the cook. One day I told the cook that I was having a birthday soon.

"And when will that be, young miss?" he asked me.

I told him.

"And how old will you be then?"

"Nine," I answered proudly.

"My, my! What a big girl you are!" He patted me on the head.

My birthday fell out on a Shabbos. What a surprise we had when, in the middle of our Shabbos meal, the cook walked out of the kitchen with an elaborate birthday cake. As he approached our table, he announced to all the diners that a young lady was celebrating her birthday today and asked everyone to get up and sing "Happy Birthday." Well, that was a surprise! Afterward he set the cake down on the table, and we thanked him profusely.

After the meal a woman in a blue dress came over to me and held out a five-dollar bill. That was a lot of money in those days. I looked at my father, and he shook his head imperceptibly. The lady was waiting for me to take the money. I had no choice but to tell her that I could not take it since it was Shabbos and we were not allowed to touch money. I was afraid she would be insulted and walk away in a huff. But she said that she understood and would look for me after Shabbos.

I was sure she would not return. In my mind's eye, I could see a small fortune floating away from me. But I knew that I had no other option but to refuse to take it. I returned to the dining room at the end of Shabbos, anxiously looking for the lady in blue. Finally I spotted her. She came over to me and told me it took a lot of courage to refuse the money.

The Businessman

Eventually my father turned to the construction business, starting with small single-family homes on the oceanfront in the Bay Parkway section of Brooklyn. He did well with this enterprise and soon went on to constructing hi-rise apartment buildings. He built them in numerous locations in Brooklyn, Bronx, and Manhattan and expanded to New Jersey. He was a fair and good boss, and his employees loved him.

Once he was driving home Friday afternoon from a construction site in Long Island. It was late, and he was speeding. He was caught and given a ticket.

My father appeared in court as required. Court protocol requires removing one's head covering. Father removed his hat, but left his yarmulke in place. Apparently the judge didn't like the sight of it and when passing judgment said, "Yarmulke or no yarmulke, I fine you seventy-five dollars!"

My father was enraged. "What kind of judge are you? How dare you say such a thing to me?"

The judge was fuming as he banged his gavel loudly on the table. "For contempt of court, you must pay a one hundred fifty dollar fine!" he shouted.

"I don't care if you give me a five-hundred-dollar fine! This is a free country, and I may practice any religion I want. And you have no right to insult me publically for it!"

Father was quite prepared to go to jail in order to stand up for the honor of Heaven.

It happened often that my father would be in New Jersey on Fridays when he was building there. Sometimes, on the short winter Fridays, it was a real hassle for him to make it home in time for Shabbos. As early as he would start out on his trip back home, he would get embroiled in the terrible weekend traffic.

It was a gray and dreary day one Friday when Shabbos was rapidly approaching and Father still had not arrived home. My mother called the New Jersey office, but, of course, there was no answer. Those were the days before cellular phones, and my mother had no way of getting in touch with him. She called the police to inquire if there had been any road accidents, but they knew nothing.

The sun was setting, and it came time to light the Shabbos candles. Tearfully Mother kindled the tiny flames and spent a long time in prayer over them. She conducted the Shabbos meal with us, trying to bring in the happy spirit of Shabbos. To our queries of where Father was, she said that he was unable to come home and Hashem was watching out for him. We could see that something was wrong, but we had faith in our invincible father that things would turn out all right.

My mother put us to bed and then stayed up saying *tehillim*. It was raining heavily by then, and her anxiety was great. *Where could he be? Why didn't he call? Does he have anything to eat?* The thoughts went around and around in her head.

Finally, at about midnight, there was a knock at the door. My mother opened it to a very wet and bedraggled husband, a puddle of water collecting around his feet. Her eyes filled with tears as she took in the sorry sight.

"Oh, *baruch Hashem*, you are home in one piece!" she cried out in relief as she ushered him into the warmth of the house. My mother managed to keep her curiosity at bay while my father changed his clothes and drank a cup of hot tea. Then he told her what happened.

"The traffic was terrible. On the bridge between New Jersey and New York, we were stuck bumper to bumper, barely moving. I kept my eyes on the sun and realized how low it was getting in the sky. I wanted to find a place to park and call you, but it was impossible to get out of the traffic jam. Finally I managed to get off the bridge and park the car. I emptied my pockets, locked the car, and put the keys under a stone nearby. I prayed to Hashem that I get home unharmed and began walking. I had no idea how long it would take, but I did not know any place to stop on the way home so I just kept going.

"I hadn't eaten anything for a number of hours and was very thirsty. I felt that if I wouldn't drink something I would collapse, so I stopped at a candy store and asked the man for a glass of water.

"The man said, 'Five cents, mister.'

" 'Look, sir,' I said to him, 'you know what is the Sabbath, the holy Sabbath?'

"He nodded.

" 'I got stuck in traffic and couldn't get home before the Sabbath started at sundown. I had to leave my car and start walking home because we don't drive on the Sabbath. I left my money and all of my possessions in the car because we are not allowed to conduct business or touch money on our day of rest. I haven't eaten or drunk anything for hours, and I still have a few hours ahead of me before I get home. I must have a drink before I collapse. I promise I will bring you the money after the Sabbath ends.'

"The man refused. I went from candy store to candy store, begging for a drink of water, but to no avail. Finally, there was one store owner who seemed a little more decent than the rest. The man looked skeptical. He had probably never heard of such a thing in his life.

" 'Funny way to spend your day of rest, walking for hours,' he said as he pushed the glass of water over to me. I finished it in a few gulps, and he filled the glass a second and a third time. I guess he figured he could give away a couple of glasses of water for nothing. Then he softened a little and asked me if I wanted something to eat.

" 'I can't eat anything you have here because I eat only kosher food. But the water made me feel a lot better. Thank you, sir. You will see. I will bring you what I owe you after the Sabbath when I come to get the car.'

" 'That's all right, mister. Hope you get home safe and sound.'

"I knew I must pay him, even though he wanted no payment. I didn't want him to think that Jews are *shnorers.*

"I continued on my way, much refreshed. The man stood there, looking after me with a quizzical expression on his face. He must have been wondering if he would ever see me again. Then it started raining. It was raining hard, but I didn't want to stop in a doorway or under a building. I just wanted to get home as fast as possible."

Father was exhausted after his ordeal and soaked through and through. But he insisted on eating his Shabbos meal and singing all of the Shabbos *zemiros* as usual. In the morning we were thrilled to see him, but we had taken it for granted that he would come home.

After Shabbos Father made Havdalah and sang his *motza'ei Shabbos zemiros* hurriedly. Mother asked him what the rush was. He answered that he wished to pay the man for the water as soon as he could to show him that Jews keep their word. He took a taxi to the place where he had parked the car on Friday. To his good fortune the car was there, untouched. He quickly drove over to the candy store where he had gotten the drink.

"Hello, I came to pay you for the water."

"What? It's really you? I don't believe it!" The man was touched and happy to see how my father kept his word. This was another *kiddush Hashem* to Father's record.

One time he had a much more serious ordeal. He was driving home one Friday on the highway when he lost control of the car, and it collided with a tree. My mother was called from the hospital where he had been brought unconscious. *Baruch Hashem,* the car was destroyed instead of him. It was a total wreck, but he recovered fully.

My father said he did not remember crashing into the

tree. An eyewitness said he saw the car swerve before it crashed, and he thought that my father was sleeping or drunk. The doctors believed he might have lost consciousness before he actually crashed. Numerous tests were made, but the doctors could not find the cause of the problem. It might have been overwork and exhaustion.

Father desperately wanted to go home for Shabbos, but the doctors refused to release him. On Sunday he called a taxi and left without asking permission. Hashem saved him from a catastrophe, but the accident was a warning to him to slow down. He did slow down while he was recovering, but soon enough he got right back into his normal routine, although he did not resume driving after that.

Despite the difficulties, the construction business might have been a very profitable enterprise if not for two major problems: the unions and the police.

The unions were corrupt and used their power to extract enormous demands from the employers. In those days people worked a six-day week and were off on Sundays. Of course, my father would not consider building on Shabbos, not even to leave the work under the charge of his foreman. There was no construction done on Shabbos on Father's building sites.

This situation was unheard of in the union's book. One day a union official approached my father. He told him that what he was doing to the men was unacceptable.

"Mr. Rabinowicz," he said, "either our men work six days a week or you pay them for six days. And if you do not comply with our demands, you can be sure that you will never find anyone to work for you again for the rest of your sojourn on this earth."

The men let my father know that if he was thinking of going to the police with a complaint against them, he would be in for a big surprise. No one was going to fight the big union bosses!

My father realized he was up against a very powerful foe. He consulted other religious Jewish builders. They suggested he do what many businesses did with *chametz* on Pesach: "Sell it to a goy." They would "sell the business to a goy" for Shabbos and allowed construction to continue as during the week.

My father would not rely on a leniency like that. He had no choice but to acquiesce to the union boss and pay his workers six days' wages for a five-day week. When he had a small enterprise with a small number of workers, he might have been able to cover the extra cost and still make a profit. But now he was employing hundreds of workers for the construction of the high-rise buildings. For many years he paid for six days of work when he received only five days of labor in return.

There was another impossible demand that the union made on my father. My father refused to operate during Chol HaMo'ed. There is room to be lenient if the building isn't being built for Jews, and it is outside the *techum Shabbos* (a distance of two thousand cubits) of the Jewish community, and the loss is a substantial one for the builder. But, as with building on Shabbos, my father was not looking for loopholes in the halachah and decided not to build during Chol HaMo'ed.

As expected, the union bosses were furious. My father was laying off their men for as much as four or five working days. They demanded that he give them an equal amount of Sundays to work at double overtime rates. If he refused, he would never find a laborer to work for him ever again. Father had no choice but to agree.

Then the union boss decided that even that concession wasn't good enough. They demanded an additional ten or fifteen Sundays at double overtime rates as compensation for having to work on their day of rest. If that wasn't enough, the union found numerous reasons to strike. They were squeezing the blood out of my father bit by bit, slowly but surely.

There were times when Father tried to fight the union's unreasonable demands. He didn't realize the folly of such an approach. It happened once, when he was walking on the building site, a concrete block fell off the building and nearly hit him. He was being informed, not very delicately, that one did not argue with the "big bosses."

Another exasperating challenge was dealing with the police. They constantly patrolled construction sites, giving out fines for any and every imaginable offense, such as leaving rubble on the street and interfering with traffic. They openly demanded money in exchange for "looking away" during inspections. If not for the large bribes they were given regularly, they would fabricate reasons for issuing huge fines.

My father's foreman, Frank, was a very honest and dedicated worker. Tall and rugged with a charming smile and sparkling blue eyes, he had immigrated to America from Scandinavia. My father trusted him completely.

One day Frank came over to his boss visibly upset. "I'm fed up, Mike! Can't work here anymore. I'm going back to my country!"

"Why, Frank? What happened?" my father asked him with real concern. It couldn't be about the foreman's wages; Frank was earning a hefty salary.

"You won't believe this, Mike! A police officer came to me and told me that whenever I order things like air conditioners I should order an extra one. He told me that I order so many anyway that one more won't be noticed. When the order comes in, I should give him the extra one! And, he tells me, if I don't do what he wants, I will have plenty of trouble from him! What is this? This is not a democratic country!"

My father tried to calm him down. "Don't worry, Frank. We won't give in. I'm going to go to the chief of police and tell him about it. They'll stop it! You'll see."

I don't know if the chief of police managed to stop it or not, but I'm sure that my father incurred many extra fines as a result of his resolve. It could not be helped. He was not a man to give in to corruption.

Despite the difficulties, my father built more and more, expanding into many different areas in and around New York. A major accomplishment of my father's was the construction of a large commerce building in Camden, New Jersey. The luncheon that celebrated the official opening of the building was attended by the mayor and other city officials. Although he spoke with an accent, Father delivered a welcoming address in perfect English. His sense of humor was apparent as he opened his address with the following joke.

"Two American Jews were once touring Germany. One of them sneezed, and a passerby said, '*Gezundheit.*'

"Oh, thank you!" the American exclaimed. "I didn't know they speak English in Germany!"

My father was trying to make his audience feel comfortable with his Yiddish accent by pointing out that lots of Yiddish words had become part of the English vernacular.

My father was always respectful of others. He tried his

best to iron out difficulties in a manner that was satisfactory to all parties. He made a point of showing his appreciation to the people he dealt with, and as a result they always felt good around him. Once, when he was on vacation in Florida, he sent the bank manager of the Camden Trust Company a basket of fruit and delectables. The manager wrote a letter of thanks. He appreciated that my father had thought of him even on his vacation.

When my father required letters of introduction or letters of credit, he obtained them easily from the bank managers with whom he dealt. They respected him and found him entirely trustworthy. The manager of Chemical Bank wrote in one such letter, "Mr. Rabinowicz is highly regarded by us as a trustworthy and reliable individual and has always maintained his accounts in a satisfactory manner." In another letter, a bank manager wrote of my father, "Our relations with Mr. Rabinowicz have always been of a pleasant nature, and we have found him to be very reliable and of good character."

Bankruptcy

Despite the warm relationships my father cultivated in the world of business and the magnificent structures he constructed, the losses accumulated insidiously. He began feeling them more and more, and he fell deeper and deeper into debt trying to keep his business afloat.

Finally the debts ballooned to the point that my father had no choice but to declare bankruptcy. He lost his beautiful buildings to the bank. I remember this well because when I was in high school, I used to keep the records of his rent payments.

The year was 1964. I became engaged that year, just as he was going through this traumatic time in his life. Despite it all, he kept his word and gave us everything he had promised in the engagement agreement. In the first few years after I married, he still had some of his buildings. But after a while he lost them all.

My father had to undergo various court cases. The creditors approached my father, asking him not to declare bankruptcy. When bankruptcy is declared, the bank takes over all the assets of the business, keeping whatever money comes in for itself and never giving the creditors what is owed them. If, on the other hand, one declares Chapter Eleven, the bank manages the property for the business and any money coming in goes to the creditors. The creditors knew that if Mr. Rabinowicz could possibly pay them back he would want to do just that.

And that, indeed, is what happened. When my father started a new business and began earning a profit again, he paid back all of his old debts to the very last cent, even though he was absolved by law from doing so. One of his creditors, a window man, had died in the interim. My father made a special effort to find his widow and give her what he had owed her husband. Needless to say, the *kiddush Hashem* he created was boundless.

Getting out of the construction business was like getting out of a deep, dark hole. Happily my father was able to start a new enterprise that was profitable and pleasant.

Prior to declaring Chapter Eleven and losing all of his buildings, Father had tried out a different business and managed to put aside some money, so we were not destitute when he lost all of his real estate. It must have been a blow to his pride; he was a person who was used to succeeding in his endeavors. But how could he possibly foresee the stranglehold the union would exert on his business? And who else, in those days in America, would willingly pay an extra day's salary for hundreds of employees for many years as an outcome of his faithfulness to his Creator's will?

When Father came upon hard times and declared Chapter Eleven, many things changed for him. He had always been a very generous man, and he had always given to others with an open hand. Now that he was no longer a man of means he was forced to do certain things out of necessity that he normally would never have done. One example involved his being a guarantor to the bank on the Boro Park mikveh's mortgage.

When the Boro Park mikveh opened, a number of people promised regular financial support for the mikveh's upkeep. But times changed, and so did the supporters' financial status. They had to renege on their commitments. The mikveh was never a self-sufficient project, and when the financial support was discontinued, the mikveh was unable to pay its bills.

When a public place such as a mikveh cannot meet its mortgage payments, the bank cannot take it over or sell it since it belongs to the public. In such a situation, the bank will collect its liability from the guarantors.

When the mikveh was established, my father had signed for something like ten thousand dollars as liability to the bank, a fortune in those days. He never imagined that the mikveh would fall upon such dire times and fail to meet its financial responsibilities.

Since he was one of the guarantors, the bank demanded payment from my father. But he was going through his own financial crisis and was unable to meet his commitment, although legally he was responsible to do so. He had no choice but to go collecting, asking people for donations for the mikveh. He managed to raise about half the amount he had signed for.

It was a major blow to my father not to be able to meet his commitments. The tremendous pressure changed him in some way.

One Sunday morning my father knocked on our tenant's door. He told Yoel Weiss that he wanted to charge him for parking in the driveway, something he hadn't done till then. The two of them couldn't settle on a price that was satisfactory to both, and Mr. Weiss decided to rent a different driveway. This involved a great inconvenience for him, since the closest one he could find was one and a half blocks away.

After a while, when Father saw that he hadn't found a tenant for his driveway, he offered Mr. Weiss the option of parking there again for the rent he had been willing to pay. Mr. Weiss refused his offer. Then Father told him he could come back for free. Mr. Weiss explained that he had a lease on the other driveway, and he had to remain there. My father felt badly about the way things had developed, especially since the other driveway was so far away. He told his tenant to come back for nothing, and he would pay off the remainder of his lease on the other driveway! That was an offer Mr. Weiss could not refuse.

After my father was established and set up in his new business, he kept apologizing to Mr. Weiss for having wanted to charge him the rent. Mr. Weiss understood that he had done it only because he had fallen on hard times. He wouldn't judge him on this one incident in which he had acted out of unusual pressure. He knew this was not his landlord's real nature.

Yoel Weiss started looking for a house to buy since his three-year lease was drawing to a close. My father asked him to stay on and promised that he wouldn't increase the rent. Mr. Weiss offered to pay my father an extra fifty dollars a month, but Father refused even that. The Weisses stayed for another half year until they made the closing on the house they eventually bought. Needless to say, they parted from my parents on very good terms.

The Export Business

My father started exporting bicycles, radios, tools, air conditioners, and small appliances to islands such as Barbados, the Caribbean, and the West Indies. Our finished basement, used for Torah and *kedushah* on Shabbos and holidays, was the office for the new export business, Good Planning & Trading Corp., established in 1967. How he learned a new business at this stage of his life is beyond me. But his resolve was as strong as ever, and master it he did!

My mother took the orders and did the bookkeeping at first until the business grew. Then he hired secretaries and a bookkeeper. His customers in the West Indies and the Caribbean were very fond of him, and he always treated them with respect and warmth.

My father traveled often to the islands to get orders and build up the business, bringing with him heavy catalogues and samples in his briefcase. The doctors had forbidden him to carry heavy things; he suffered greatly from his eyes and carrying heavy weights was contraindicated. As a child, he had contracted an eye disease that left scarring on his retinas. His sight had always been very poor, but even so he learned extensively every day. Eventually his eyesight deteriorated to the degree that he was considered legally blind. But this never stopped Father from doing what he had to do.

He also suffered for many years from gastrointestinal problems. On his trips, he usually ate only the matzah and sardines he brought along with him, since obtaining kosher food on the islands was impossible. He was very stringent with the laws of kashrus and would not even drink milk from the islands since it was not *chalav Yisrael.* Instead, Mother sent powdered milk along with him.

Plane connections between the islands were poor and far between. Sometimes my father would spend long hours waiting for his connecting flights. He spent so many of his precious hours traveling, but he always had *sefarim* with him, and he was able to learn at any odd moment. His business probably would have benefited more had he spent more time on the islands to obtain more orders and spent less on travel expenses. But it was important to him to spend Shabbos with the family and to give his Shabbos *shiur,* so he never considered staying away from home over Shabbos. Later on in his life, once the children were all out of the house, my mother went along with him occasionally so that he could stay over the weekend. And sometimes they even took along one of Boruch's children, Yossi or Rivky, as a treat.

My father's being an observant Jew led to some humorous incidents on his travels. Often the customs officials were stumped when viewing the contents of his suitcase. The natives had never seen the religious objects he often took along with him.

On one of my mother's trips to the islands with Father,

she was witness to a funny incident involving a shofar. During the month of Elul Father blew the shofar every morning, a common custom in many Jewish communities. This is done in an attempt to arouse oneself to repentance in the days leading up to the *Yamim Nora'im*, the Days of Awe. The customs official did not know what the twisted ram's horn was.

"What's this?" he asked.

"It's part of my religion." My father's usual answer.

"What ya mean? This is no Bible."

The man looked suspicious, turning it this way and that. He took out a long implement and tried to poke it into the open end of the shofar. It didn't go in very far due to the shofar's convoluted contours.

"Explain what ya mean. What ya need it for?"

"You use it to pray to God. Like you are begging Him for help."

But the man was sure there was some contraband hidden inside. He poked the shofar's depths more vigorously, pushing first from the top and then from the bottom. My father was getting impatient, but the man was intent on finding something. He called over some of his colleagues, and they put their heads together over the mystery.

"Oh, I know," one of them said. "He drinks wine from it."

"Ya fool!" the other responded. "How can ya drink wine from it when it is open at both ends?"

When one of them left and came back with a hammer, my father put his foot down. "Look, gentlemen," he said with as much grace and diplomacy as he could muster, "let me show you how we use the shofar when we pray to God."

He took his precious possession from the customs official's hands, put it to his lips, and let forth a piercing blast.

The men trembled, thinking perhaps that he had called down God's wrath upon them. They pushed my father's things over to him.

"Okay, sir. We understand now. You're a musician!"

"Yes, of course. And I use the shofar to pray with every day before our New Year's holiday. Good day, gentlemen."

He gathered up his luggage and made a hurried departure before they changed their minds. After that incident, my mother always gave my father a Jewish calendar to take along, one that had a picture of a Jew swathed in a tallis blowing a shofar.

That day, as a result of the delay caused by customs in their examination of the shofar, my father realized that he would not get to the hotel in time to daven *minchah*, so he decided to daven at the airport. "The whole airport was about as big as our dining room," Mother told us. My father could not find a private spot in which to pray, so he chose a spot under a tree.

As a chassidic Jew, Father always davened wearing a *gartel*. Sometimes he did not have one handy when he needed it. He would then produce a makeshift *gartel* by, for example, tying two handkerchiefs together. On this occasion he had no time to get the *gartel* out of his suitcase, so he used his tie instead and proceeded to daven *Shemoneh Esrei*, oblivious to the commotion around him.

Milling about were many other plane passengers, native women and children with live chickens and geese and baskets full of produce that they had purchased in the market on one of the other islands. They were waiting for their husbands to pick them up and take them home. The women and children stared at the "holy man" in fascination. They formed a circle around him with their honking geese and baskets. One small child pulled his mother's shawl off her shoulders and tied it around his waist. The women and children moved their lips in silent prayer as Father did, copying his every step and bow reverently.

When the husbands finally appeared on the scene, they tried to get their wives' attention, honking their horns and yelling, "Come! Come!" It was as though they did not exist; the women would not budge. The men were made to wait patiently until my father took his last three steps backward, bowing to the left, then to the right, and then to the center, then taking three steps forward and bouncing three times in place, while the women and children faithfully copied his every move. Only when he finished did they disperse. My mother heard some of the women saying, "Oh, he's a good man! A good man! He talks to God!"

My father had been oblivious to it all. By the time he turned around, the crowd was gone. When Father came over to Mother, she burst out in loud, hysterical laughter.

"Do you know what was going on while you were davening?" she asked him.

"No, of course not. How would I know what was going on when I was focused on talking to Hashem!"

She described the comic scene that had just taken place, and he had a good laugh, too.

Finally they headed for their hotel. Each morning Father pushed himself into the closet of their room, deep among the clothes, and blew his shofar. Despite the fact that the sound was muffled, it still escaped the confines of the closet. The poor natives had no idea what it was. They were terrified, thinking that it was an air-raid siren or the signal of some other disaster coming down on them!

My father once had to deal with a grave situation when the customs official wanted to cut open his tefillin to see what they contained. They were sure he was hiding contraband inside. My father told the man, "Why don't you ask the local rabbi? He'll tell you what it is."

"We don't have any rabbi here."

My father persuaded them not to damage the tefillin by showing them the calendar my mother sent along with the picture of a Jew wearing tallis and tefillin.

On another occasion, Father was learning on the veranda of the hotel. A man came over to him and introduced himself. He was the Minister of Education of that particular island.

"What are you studying?" he asked.

My father was learning Gemara. He replied, "This is our Bible."

The man nodded knowingly.

"Do you learn the Bible, too?" my father asked him.

"Oh, certainly. As a matter of fact, I even give sermons on the Bible, although I am not a preacher." The man beamed proudly.

"That's just wonderful!"

"Mr. Rabinowicz, I would be most honored if you'd come to hear my sermon tomorrow at our local church. We begin at eleven o'clock." He waited expectantly for a response.

My father thought quickly and answered, "How kind of you. I would love to come. I'm sure you give a very enlightening sermon. The problem is that when I am on my travels I have so little time to spend on each of the islands before I must return home. I am always so pressured for time that I can never manage to see all of my customers. One day, when I have more free time, I will be very happy to attend your sermon."

His answer seemed to satisfy the man, and they parted on excellent terms.

On another of Father's trips to the Caribbean, a woman approached him.

"Hello, my name is Helen Stein.* Are you a rabbi?" she asked.

"No, I'm not a rabbi, but I am an observant Jew. Can I help you with something?" he asked her kindly.

"Perhaps you can. I am a Jew but not at all religious. I am thinking about marrying someone who is not Jewish. We really get on very well. What do you think about that?"

"Each kind mixes well with its own kind. Think about the influence your marrying a non-Jew will have upon yourself, on your family and friends, and on your future children. Think of the larger picture."

"But it's nearly impossible to meet young Jewish people here," she countered.

"If you sincerely wish to do the right thing, God will see that it happens. Just put your trust and faith in Him."

"Well, thank you," she replied pensively. "I'll think about what you said." They parted ways, and my father soon forgot about the incident.

One day, about six months later, Father heard someone calling him.

"Hi, Mr. Rabinowicz! I've been looking for you. Do you remember me?"

He dug into his memory and recalled his encounter with this young woman.

"Hello, Helen. Good to see you."

"I'm so glad I've met you. I wanted to thank you for your advice! I reconsidered marrying my non-Jewish boyfriend. Amazingly, I met a Jewish man shortly after speaking to you, and we fit perfectly. We are happily married, thank God. I was hoping to meet you so that I could thank you."

"Good for you, Helen!" my father replied enthusiastically. "I'm glad it worked out so well for you! Best of luck to you both."

He was really happy for her. And he really cared when he gave her advice. It was this sincerity that impressed people and allowed him to help them.

As hard as it was, with the frequent traveling, the grueling flight schedules, the heavy catalogues and inadequate meals, my father succeeded in building up his export enterprise until it was a profitable business. He had very good relationships with the people he dealt with. The Minister of Health of one of the islands often visited the United States, and he'd visit Father's basement office. He found the secretaries very helpful; they even went shopping for imports with him on the East Side of New York.

The Minister of Health once came to visit on a Friday. They treated him as a special guest, serving him tea with cake. Mr. Tomohu* was not in a great hurry, and he lingered there, making small talk. He had no idea that it was nearly Shabbos for Mr. Rabinowicz. The minute hand was getting closer and closer to the time of candle lighting, and the man seemed to have no intention of leaving. Finally my mother had to go upstairs to light candles.

She came back down, and my father said, "Excuse me, Mr. Tomohu, I must change my clothes. It is now the start of our Sabbath, and I must leave shortly for the synagogue."

"Is that so, sir? Go right ahead." My father left the room, and Mr. Tomohu turned to my mother. "Your husband is going to his synagogue. That sounds most interesting. I would like to see this synagogue of his. I think I will join him."

Mother was taken aback. She didn't think it would be very appropriate for Father to go to shul with a black Christian in tow.

"Oh, Mr. Tomohu," she said, "I don't think it is worth your while to go to the synagogue this week. This is just a regular Sabbath and not very interesting. You must come when we have a festival. That's when it really gets interesting. You know what? The next time we celebrate a festival we will call you to come."

Luckily Mother's logic convinced him. My father returned to the office in full Shabbos regalia, in his shiny *bekeshe* and *shtreimel.* Father said that since he had to go to synagogue very shortly, he would call a taxi to take Mr. Tomohu back to his hotel.

When the taxi arrived, my father escorted his client outside. They made quite a spectacle for the Boro Park crowd, Father in his Shabbos best and the black man towering over him. They looked at my father in amazement, wondering what he was busy with a few minutes before Shabbos.

Mr. Tomohu was a good customer and a decent person. Some years after this incident my parents heard that he had been killed in an uprising on the island.

My father was away on his travels most of the week, and it was the secretaries who actually conducted the day-to-day affairs of the business. They would prepare their list of questions for the boss, and Mother would get the answers when talking with him.

Before Shabbos the desks would be pushed over to the side and tables and chairs set up for his *shiur*. My mother covered the typewriters and telex machine with tablecloths in honor of Shabbos.

When he decided to sell the business, Father advertised for a buyer. Someone answered the ad who was seriously interested in buying the business. My father suggested that he come along with him to the islands to see how the business was run. The man agreed.

They landed on one of the islands at night, and my father sat down to learn. There was no minyan on the island, so he davened in the hotel, and then they went to sleep. The next morning they davened, and my father learned for another few hours. After that they ate lunch, and then finally my father said that they should go and do some business.

They went to see one of Father's customers. The man had a whole list of complaints. Father kept saying only, "Good. We'll take care of it. Don't worry. We'll see to it...," and so on. And then he said, "But what else do you need? How many refrigerators do you need? How many stoves do you need?" Although the customer was still complaining, he was giving my father an order. The prospective buyer of the business watched the scene in amazement.

To get around, one had to fly from island to island. My father and the man who was interested in buying the business left the first island and flew to the next one. As they went from customer to customer, the prospective buyer grew more and more astonished. The customers were all complaining, yet they were still ordering!

At the end of the day my father's guest could hold out no longer. "They're complaining, but they're still buying!"

"Of course they're buying. They have no one else to buy from. No one else comes to these islands to sell to them. No matter how much they complain, they still have to buy."

They went back to the hotel to eat supper, and then my father sat down to learn again. In all that time they worked about five or six hours. My father probably learned more that day than he'd worked.

A day or two later they returned to the States. The man told Father that he would think things over. When he got back to my father, he said, "I'm sorry. Your kind of livelihood is *l'ma'alah min hateva,* outside the realm of normal. I don't think I merit that kind of divine intervention. This business is not for me." He couldn't comprehend how my father could learn so much and still make money.

Eventually Father found a buyer. The secretaries were heartbroken when my father sold the business and actually cried when it came time to part company with him.

Mr. Kraus* became the new proprietor of Good Planning & Trading Corp., and Father spent about a year of his time, without any recompense, teaching the man the ins and outs of it. He even traveled with him to all of his customers.

The secretaries tried working for the new boss, but it wasn't the same as before. Mr. Kraus was not cut out for this type of business. His former customers complained, "Mr. Rabinowicz, what did you do? We had such a good relationship with you. You killed the business!" My father had tried to pass his enterprise over intact, but it just wasn't meant to be.

Father managed to save enough money from the sale of his export business to buy an apartment in Eretz Yisrael, help my sister buy an apartment, and even put away money in savings for various Torah projects.

A Man of the Community

Wherever my father found himself, he always threw himself into community affairs. If something needed to be taken care of, he was the first to make sure it was done. When my parents moved to Boro Park, my father became well known almost immediately as a *ba'al tzedakah* and a very dynamic community activist. He was always asked to head committees and be the guest of honor at various fund-raising dinners.

My father was so involved in community affairs that he spent a lot of time out of the house. But he was still our father and we knew it. When we were children, he made sure to be home every Shabbos even when he was running his export business and had to travel a lot. The attention he gave us on

Shabbos was one sign of his devotion to us. When we grew older and married, my parents made sure to never miss a family *simchah*. They even attended the brisos of all the grandchildren, no matter where they were — whether in Lakewood, Monsey, or Bnei Brak. Avigayil lived perhaps the most far away of all of us, yet still my father managed to make it to the brisos of her children.

Abby married Alan Wedderkopp, an English mining engineer. Since Alan worked in the North Sea, they made their first home in Norway. Abby recalls how our father and mother came for the bris of both of her boys, once to Norway and once to Newcastle, England.

They were living in a tiny hamlet in the Norwegian mountains, in an old schoolhouse. The hamlet had a population of less than one hundred. The locals were simple people who rarely left the village, and then they went no further than the "big" city of Stavanger. Into this reclusive environment came my father, replete with *bekeshe* and *shtreimel* and with an imported Danish *rav* to perform the bris. My father was friendly and respectful, and long after he and my mother left, Abby's neighbors, who were good and decent people, spoke of my father with affection.

During the few days that my father and mother were in Norway, Alan's father and stepmother were there as well. Despite the apparent lack of common ground between them all, my father took a genuine interest in Fred. He gave them one of his inventions, which they treasured. It was a small radio set inside a knight's helmet. In order to operate the radio, one raised the visor on the helmet.

My father and mother also went to Benjamin's bris in Newcastle. That was a less difficult and less complicated trip

Me in front of 70 Teignmouth Road years later

My parents in front of 70 Teignmouth Road in London, my mother holding me and Abby standing

Mother and Father shortly after their marriage in England

Mother and Father years later at their grandson's wedding in New York

Bubby Schorr holding me and my baby brother Boruch, with Abby standing next to her, in London

Left to right: Bubby Schorr, Aunt Polly, Aunt Malkele, and Father, in London

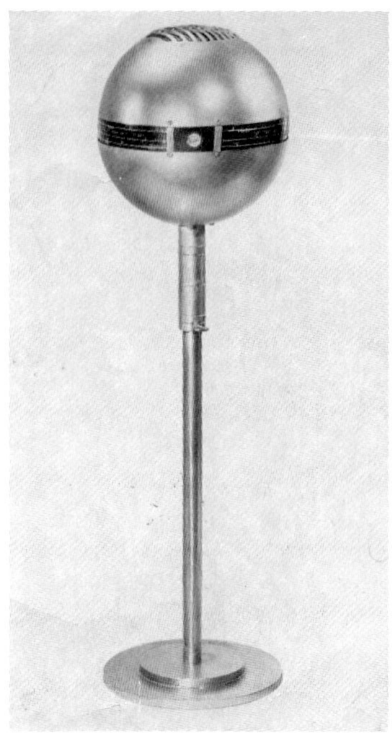

Father's invention, the Emor radio sensation of the world!

Left to right: Victor Zhitto, Abby, Mother, and Toshe, in London

The hostel boys from Chase Terrace, England. Gus Meyer is in the second row, third from the right; Joe Fertig, second row, farthest to the right; Eliezer Freifeld, first row, farthest to the left.

A testimonial dinner for Bais Yaakov of Boro Park honoring my parents. Mr. Landau, the administrator, is standing. Seated, from left to right: Mr. Israel Feigenbaum, president; Father; my uncle, Rabbi Aharon Arak; Rabbi Ehrenreich, the principal.

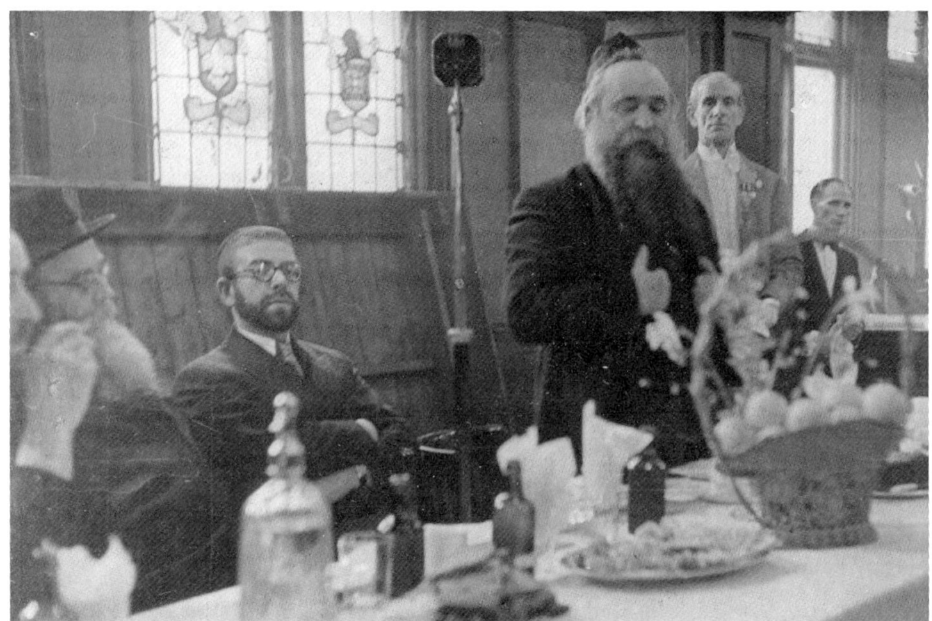

Father, with Rav Yechezkel Abramsky to his left, at a *tzedakah* function in London

Boruch's bar mitzvah. Father is standing behind his brother-in-law Rav Aharon Arak; to his right is Uncle Moishele, the Chuster Rebbe; to the Rebbe's right is Father's brother, Reb Dovid Yitzchok Isaac, the Skolyer Rebbe.

Me and Abby

Standing: Perele; from left to right: Abby, Chavi, and Boruch

Boruch, Abby, Perele, Father, and Chavi celebrating Purim in Boro Park

Father dancing with his grandson at his wedding in Bnei Brak, Reb Yudel Shapiro in the background

Father dancing at Boruch's bar mitzvah in Boro Park

for them compared to the trip to Norway, but it was still remarkable. Although, perhaps, only a man such as he, who had a grueling work schedule and uncompromising learning *seder*, yet still made time for his family, could make such a difference to the community.

The Sefardishe Shul

Father became a member of the Sefardishe shul, formally known as First Congregation Anshei Sefard. It was a large, imposing building with pillars in the front and a tall metal fence all around it. There were two minyanim in the shul, one upstairs and one downstairs.

My father preferred to daven in the less pretentious shul downstairs. Rabbi Pinsky, an older *rav*, presided over this minyan. Although it was not a chassidic minyan, and it was considerably smaller than the upstairs congregation, my father was drawn to Rabbi Pinsky, and they became fast friends. It was here that he was invited to daven *shacharis* on the *Yamim Nora'im*. His davening was so special that one of the upstairs *rabbanim* came down especially to hear it. Although several decades have passed since I sat in shul hearing my father's *tefillos*, my davening on the *Yamim Nora'im* seems lacking if I don't pray with his beautiful melodies.

Eventually Father was elected vice president, and later president, of the shul. He was so much a part of it, and the congregation related to him as one of the key figures of the shul. They also felt a tremendous appreciation for all that he did for them, including the large donations he contributed.

Ohel Children's Home

One of my father's first projects in the United States was establishing a proper children's home for Jewish children. While Father lived in England, he was deeply affected by the plight of the many orphans of the war. His involvement with the boys' hostel made him sensitive to what those homeless children had to endure. After the war, when my father realized that all of his and my mother's siblings had been saved miraculously from the claws of Hitler, *yemach shemo*, he vowed to give fifteen percent of his earnings for charity instead of the usual ten percent. This money would be used exclusively to help Jewish children in unfortunate circumstances.

In the early 1960s he placed an ad in the paper, stating that anyone who had any connection with Jewish orphans should contact him immediately for financial assistance. A Rabbi Yaakov Weiss came forward. Rabbi Weiss explained the current situation in the United States regarding the existing Jewish children's homes. There was no children's home that catered to the religious Jewish child.

Rabbi Weiss, himself an orphan, understood the lack in the existing facilities only too well. Orphaned Jewish children, children from broken homes, or disabled Jewish children who could not be raised by their own parents were put into homes established by the Jewish Federation. The Jewish Federation orphanage that Weiss had lived in as a boy did not provide anything Jewish for the children; they were raised in a completely secular atmosphere. There was no kashrus or Shabbos or *yom tov*. These homes sent the children to public schools, and the children had no way of obtaining a Jewish education.

At that time Rabbi Weiss was involved with helping Mrs. Batsheva Mandel and a small group of people to create an Orthodox Jewish children's home. They were having little success getting the project off the ground. My father told Rabbi Weiss that he would happily contribute money to the cause, but he did not have enough to establish a children's home. But he promised to convene a meeting and explain the situation to the Jews in his community.

This was the start of another major undertaking of my father's life. Rabbi Weiss moved to Eretz Yisrael very shortly after that initial meeting with my father, and they didn't actually work together on founding Ohel. But he was the catalyst in getting my father involved.

My father was as good as his word and organized a meeting subsequent to speaking with Rabbi Weiss. Mr. David Turkel, who served as president of Agudath Israel for many years, and other influential people attended. Immediately they raised enough money to get the project started. It seemed a matter of fact that my father would be elected president of the committee.

The first obstacle was the Jewish Federation itself. The Jewish Federation was a very large and powerful organization. They had tremendous influence in government circles. And it was not in their best interests that an Orthodox Jewish children's home be established.

Since 1962 Mrs. Batsheva Mandel had worked on getting approval for the charter of her planned home, without success. This was a necessary step in fund-raising for a nonprofit charitable organization. After having the charter approved, they would need to obtain a license for operating the children's home, without which it could not get underway. In the years she worked to open up a children's home, she was also busy placing children in foster homes, since some of them were in desperate need of care. Sometimes she was able to arrange government funding for the care of the children, where the government paid the foster parents directly.

Mrs. Mandel had named her proposed project The American Jewish Children's Home. Her lawyer took the home's charter to the Supreme Court of New York in Manhattan. It seemed that the presiding judge was affiliated with the Jewish Federation.

"What do you need a Jewish children's home for?" he asked the lawyer. "The Jewish Federation has homes. We have Jewish child-care agencies. You don't need it. I'm not approving this."

This stand-off went on for years. Appeal after appeal was made but to no avail. Once my father was apprised of the situation he immediately joined forces with Mrs. Mandel's group. Now things began moving! My father suggested changing the name of the organization and that they approach a different judge. Thus was born Ohel Children's Home.

This new battle in my father's life was strikingly similar to the battle he had fought with the Bnai Brith in England. He had to devise a plan to outwit the powerful Jewish Federation, which, unfortunately, was working so hard to prevent this children's home from coming into existence.

My father did some investigating. A black judge who worked in the court system seemed promising. Father arranged to have a hearing with him.

"Your honor," he said, "do you know what it means to belong to a minority group?"

The judge laughed. "Mr. Rabinowicz, you are talking to a minority man, as you can see."

"Well, then, your honor, you can relate to what we are going through. As religious Jews, we, too, are a minority."

He explained what the Jews had suffered over the centuries as a result of their religion. He told the judge how inconceivable it was that in twentieth-century America, in a land of democracy and freedom of religion, it was so difficult for Jewish orphans and children of broken homes to receive the proper care and upbringing their religion demanded.

"I know exactly what you are talking about," the judge concurred. "We had trouble when we wanted to open our neighborhood church."

"Your honor, you can inspect the existing Jewish children's homes yourself to see if they keep kosher and the Sabbath," Father concluded. "I appeal to you, sir, who knows what discrimination means and who can empathize with us, grant us the necessary permit so that we will be able to establish a proper facility for our children, a facility in which these unfortunate children can be raised according to their faith without bias and without discrimination."

Needless to say, my father got the permit. Mrs. Mandel's lawyer was amazed to see the gigantic Jewish Federation rendered helpless in stopping my father. He was convinced that had he tried to use Mr. Rabinowicz's tactic he would surely have been disbarred (the Federation would have seen to that). Mrs. Mandel felt that the way my father responded to her call for help, with such speed and determination, was magnificent. More than thirty-five years later she told me that she would never forget what he had done.

By the end of 1964, the charter for the organization of

Ohel had been approved by the city of New York and by the attorney general of New York State. Now the project required the involvement of someone from the State Department of Social Welfare. My father approached Senator William T. Conklin for his assistance.

Senator Conklin wrote a letter of introduction for my father to Mr. Peter Kasius, deputy commissioner of the State Department of Social Welfare. In the letter he described the need for the children's home to create a place where the children would have "the privilege of eating kosher food. Such provision is now lacking in so-called Orthodox institutions." He concluded that "he would be most grateful for any consideration and courtesies that Mr. Kasius could extend to him in this matter."

I have no idea if Senator Conklin knew my father personally, or if he was merely impressed with him and his mission upon meeting him, or if he just wanted to find favor in the eyes of the Orthodox Jewish voting public. But I am sure that this letter helped my father along the road in the creation of Ohel.

My father set up committees for fund-raising and for dealing with the myriad tasks that are necessary for creating a children's home. He was a very busy man, but the busier he was, the more he seemed to accomplish. Still, he needed someone who could spend much more time on establishing the home than he could. In the beginning, Mrs. Mandel served as the director of Ohel, while Father served as president of the board. Shortly after Ohel was operative, Rabbi Asher Buchsbaum became its executive director. When my father could no longer continue to invest as much time in Ohel as he had in the beginning, he relinquished the mantle of the presidency. But he continued to serve as honorary president for many years, even after moving to Eretz Yisrael.

Mrs. Mandel bought a two-story house in Boro Park. Over the next year this house was demolished and rebuilt into a comfortable and spacious children's residence in accordance with all the specifications of state law. The home was finally opened on April 27, 1969, seven years after she had embarked on the project.

The permit was given for twenty boys, ten on each floor. The quota of children was filled immediately. They ranged in age from four to fifteen. House parents were hired to live in the home as well as other personnel, such as counselors, teachers, and tutors. Most of the children went to the local yeshivos, but some were taught on the premises.

Mrs. Mandel continued to work actively for Ohel until 1972. Years later, she retired to Kiryat Telshe Stone in Eretz Yisrael. She described the exhilarating feeling she got, true *Yiddishe nachas,* when any of the early residents of the home contacted her. Most married and established families of their own.

Right from the start, Mother was involved with the domestic aspects of running the home. She galvanized her friends into action, forming an enthusiastic ladies' auxiliary, with Rose Stubenhaus, an active woman and a good organizer, as president. Mrs. Mandel called Mother frequently to bring her up-to-date on all that was going on and to discuss any problems that cropped up.

The day the home was to be inspected by the government was a busy one for the ladies. My mother and her friends got there early, washing floors, cleaning windows, and putting up curtains. The home was to provide a clean and pleasant environment as well as a warm and spiritual Jewish haven.

The children came and the work started. They went to school in Boro Park and spent the rest of their day in the home. Some of the children needed special help. The staff included Orthodox psychiatrists, psychologists, occupational therapists, and social workers.

Once, in anticipation of a government inspection, the staff prepared an especially tasty meal that was served to the children as well as to the inspectors. Upon leaving, one of them said, "Everything is so well run and clean. Your food is delicious. I'm not Jewish, but I think that from now on I will indulge in kosher cuisine!"

On Shabbos afternoons my father and mother visited Ohel, a twenty-minute walk from their home. It was important to them to see firsthand how the home was being run and to speak to the children. My mother enjoyed watching how well the staff interacted with their charges and how they conducted organized play. The children were blossoming under the warmth and care of the staff members.

Ohel Children's Home gained publicity. Once Ohel was contacted by a psychiatrist from a mental hospital in New Jersey. He told the director that there was a Jewish boy in his hospital who was being kept in the high-security section. His parents never visited him, and every once in a rare while his grandfather would come to see him. The doctor felt that the child did not belong in a mental institution and wanted to know whether Ohel might take him in. Ohel was only too willing to save the child, but there was a technical problem in making the transfer. Ohel had a license to operate in New York State, and taking in a New Jersey resident created legal difficulties because of the differences in state law.

My father decided he would go to the New Jersey facility and see what he could do. Somehow he managed to make the transfer legal, and Yonah Shalom* joined the children of Ohel.

Once Yoni was living in his new home, his grandfather stopped visiting him. Poor, abandoned child that he was, it was no wonder that Yoni was difficult to handle. Although he was not mentally ill, he had emotional problems. He answered in monosyllables, mainly sticking to a vocabulary of yes or no. Yoni never played in the well-stocked playroom as the other children did. When outside he stood alone under a tree, watching the others. He was in and out of trouble, and occasionally he stole. Several times he set a fire in his room. One of his pastimes was throwing stones at the neighbors' houses at night, breaking their windows. It was to Yoni's good fortune that people were kind to him and didn't want to get him into trouble for his misdemeanors.

Yoni was unable to learn in a regular yeshivah and attended a special school where he learned a trade. In later years he was able to work and function normally. But in the beginning he needed time to adjust to his new environment, and the staff went all out to help him.

Yoni's is just one of many stories. Ohel Children's Home was able to create a happy ending to a lot of very sad stories. Once again my father had put his heart and soul into saving Jewish children with much personal cost to himself. He was not satisfied to leave well enough alone. The results were happy children who would go on to create fine Jewish homes. Most fittingly, Ohel's logo states, "Where broken lives are mended."

There was always a need to collect funds for Ohel, since the government did not provide full coverage for their expenses. When my father rediscovered Gus Meyer, he got him involved in fund-raising for Ohel in Washington Heights. He did a fine job, too, and Ohel's board members awarded him with a plaque for his efforts. My father also got Joseph Fertig, who had also lived in the hostel in Aldridge, to do fund-raising in Elizabeth, New Jersey. The *rav* of Elizabeth was Rabbi Pinchas Teitz, and no one did anything in town without his approval. Mr. Fertig went to him and told him that Rabbi Rabinowicz had asked him to raise money in Elizabeth for Ohel. The *rav* immediately gave his approval and gave him a *berachah* for success.

When the renovated building on Fifty-eighth Street was about to open in May 1969, my father gave a talk on the Yiddish radio station WEVD. He described the facility and all of its wonderful services. He appealed to the listeners to help provide a Jewish upbringing for these children. The radio address gave Ohel the publicity that enabled it to grow and develop over the years and brought in much-needed funds.

Ohel became famous all over the United States. Over the years, Ohel Children's Home expanded into many different areas. It became renowned for its excellence and for the wide range of services it provided, serving as a model for other children's homes. Today it also provides foster care and adoption services, group residences, critical care residences, Bais Ezra community residences, a family support program, and adult community residences, housing brain-damaged and Down syndrome adults. All of this came out of that original impetus, the founding of an Orthodox Jewish children's home, through my father's initiative.

The fire in my father's heart for helping Jewish orphans spilled over into other projects. In November 1978 the charity funds of Kollel Chibas Yerushalayim of Rabbi Meir Ba'al HaNes started a special orphan fund for children in Eretz Yisrael. The project got underway due to Father's initiative.

Before moving to Eretz Yisrael in June 1984, my parents were honored at Ohel's dinner. My mother was awarded the *Eishes Chayil* plaque. Typical of Mother's humility, she was annoyed that no one had consulted her about it. She felt that since she was moving and was not so involved with Ohel anymore, she did not deserve the honor.

After moving to Eretz Yisrael, Father still served as a board member. In 1985 Ohel's executive director and president named him an honorary board member. In that capacity, they wrote, his "past and future service would serve as an inspiration worthy of emulation."

In January 1988 Father was one of the three presidents honored at Ohel's eighteenth annual dinner and awarded a plaque for his outstanding efforts on behalf of Ohel, designated with the title "master builder." My father came alone from Eretz Yisrael specially for the dinner. He spoke lovingly of the dedication of Ohel's founding leaders. "You cannot believe the difficulties we had. The original group had tremendous *mesiras nefesh*. They were people who truly were motivated only *l'sheim Shamayim* (for the sake of Heaven)." He expressed great satisfaction that the current leadership had kept Ohel dedicated entirely to the principle of *chesed*.

After the event was over, Mr. Max Wasser, the current president, sent my father a handwritten letter. "I just want you to know what great *chizuk* it was to us to have you come all the way from Eretz Yisrael to attend our dinner.... Financially it was the most successful we ever had." He enclosed an article from the *Jewish Press*, which had devoted a full page to the event.

When Max Wasser traveled to Eretz Yisrael, he visited my parents in Bayit Vegan. "Whom should we thank for Ohel if not for you?" he said to them.

After my father passed away, Mother received a letter from Bais Ezra. The writers expressed their condolences to our family and wrote, "When Rabbi Rabinowicz first founded Ohel, who could have imagined how far-reaching his *chesed* would be? One of the outgrowths of Ohel's original home for orphaned boys is its Bais Ezra program for developmentally disabled adults. Bais Ezra today services eighty adults in homes of Orthodox standards and a warm, loving environment. The happiness Bais Ezra provides for these individuals, and the relief it offers their families, is immeasurable.

"Rabbi Rabinowicz, *a"h,* can now reap his due rewards in the *olam ha'emes.* His merits continue to increase as each Jewish person in need is helped by Ohel and Bais Ezra."

Until I began researching for this book, I was not even aware that Bais Ezra was a division of Ohel. I know a very special family whose daughter lives in one of their adult housing facilities. I had no idea that it was in my father's merit that these people benefited.

Bais Yaakov of Boro Park

My father was a great supporter of the Bais Yaakov of Boro Park. My sisters and I went to elementary school there. When the board realized that they desperately needed a new building to accommodate the growing student population, they approached my father. He served as a member of their building committee, got the committee organized, and was very instrumental in the success of the project. The new building eventually accommodated twelve hundred elementary school girls!

In February of 1964, my parents consented to be Bais Yaakov's guests of honor at their testimonial dinner after the new school building was erected. The write-up on my father in the dinner invitation was very fitting. "Rabbi Mechel Rabinowicz, in the course of years, has won the respect and admiration of the Jewish community as a *talmid chacham* and a philanthropist."

Rabbi Ehrenreich, the principal of the school, said so many people did not believe the new building would ever come into existence. But my father was one of the few people who believed it would happen. Not only did he contribute to the building fund, but his knowledge from his construction business helped immensely.

In the letter of thanks that the president, Mr. Israel Feigenbaum, sent my father immediately following the dinner, he wrote (among other things): "It is most difficult to compose a 'thank you' letter with regards to your service to our school, which would convey our sincere feelings... The affair was a resounding success because the community of Boro Park felt that it was their duty and obligation to pay its respects to you, who have done so much for them."

The Boro Park Mikveh

Boro Park was fast growing into a large Jewish Orthodox community. The local mikveh was becoming inadequate to handle the growing demand. It came to a point that the clientele it served would often come home in the early morning hours. It became a dire necessity to build a new one. My father was approached by a delegation who was determined to do something about the situation.

"Mr. Rabinowicz," they said, "Boro Park is desperately in need of a new and larger mikveh. We ask you to please take charge of this project."

My father was under tremendous pressure dealing with the problems of his construction business at the time. Father tried to get out of it.

They would not be put off.

"Mr. Rabinowicz, if you will not head this vital undertaking, no one will, and Boro Park will remain without the mikveh it so desperately needs!"

My father understood that he had a responsibility to the community. He could not find it within himself to refuse them. He was chosen president of the Boro Park Mikveh building committee. Mr. Morgenstern, a wealthy man with whom my father had business dealings, gave a large contribution to the project. More importantly, he agreed to be a guarantor for the mikveh project's bank loans. This ensured the project credit with the bank.

My father was offered the job of builder of the new mikveh. He refused the offer, fearing that some might say he was making money off a *tzedakah* project. He was asked to recommend a builder. Again, he was apprehensive lest people think he had a personal interest in doing so. Instead, he supplied the committee with several names of builders and told them to investigate the merits of each and choose the one they preferred. He invested his knowledge as a builder and his drive and determination to get the job done as quickly as possible. But he refused to make money off the project despite the fact that it would have been fairly earned.

There were some struggles along the way, especially with finding the most suitable construction materials that would fit all the halachic requirements. Another problem involved the land itself. The plot of land designated for the new mikveh was situated on a huge boulder, which had to be removed completely. This was a very complicated job and one that entailed great expense. My father worked at it stubbornly until the task was done.

The plans were designed for a very large mikveh, and building it would prove to be singularly complicated. Construction had actually begun when someone discovered a problem that required that the job be started again from the beginning. My father had personal experience with building a mikveh in London. He knew how difficult it was to construct one that would not leak.

Many engineers and architects were working on the project. They could not come to a decision about the best way to build it, nor could they agree on a construction strategy. Finally, after a lot of debate, they proposed a certain type of cement that was absolutely waterproof. My father said he would go ahead with their recommendation only if the committee of *rabbanim* said that this cement was kosher. The *rabbanim* argued that making the mikveh this way was comparable to creating a vessel within a vessel, which halachically is not a kosher way of building a mikveh. Father refused to go ahead with the plans as proposed. People were becoming impatient and began complaining that they didn't have their mikveh because Mr. Rabinowicz was causing so many problems.

My father asked them, "How can I agree to something that the *rabbanim* are saying is not acceptable according to halachah? Perhaps you should get yourselves a new president."

No one could imagine doing the job without my father. It took some time, but finally all the problems were ironed out.

There were people who claimed that Father had made a lot of money on the project. This totally unfounded accusation was very painful for him, for he always exhausted himself, outdid himself, for the sake of a mitzvah.

When the Satmar Rebbe was visiting Boro Park, my father went to see him. Although he was not a Satmar chassid, he felt that it was simple courtesy to go and greet the Rebbe. Father asked him if he would honor them with a visit to the newly built mikveh. My father took him on a tour, and the Rebbe was very impressed. After studying how it was actually built, adhering to all the halachic requirements, he said it was the finest mikveh he knew of.

"Ich vill freigen the Rebbe epes — I want to ask the Rebbe something," my father said. *"Farvas iz azoi feel tzaros tzu machen a mikveh?* — Why are there so many problems with making a mikveh?"

The Rebbe answered, *"Veil a mikveh hot nisht kein mizrach!* — Because a mikveh doesn't have an eastern wall!"

In shul prominent people are honored by being given seats along the eastern wall, notifying the congregants of their special status. For honor people will put themselves all out. When there is no honor involved, the job is done with less dedication, enthusiasm, and determination.

Of course, this was not true of my father or the others who devoted so much time to this project.

Bikur Cholim

The Boro Park Bikur Cholim was in need of a facelift. Just as with the mikveh, this organization was totally inadequate for the needs of the growing community. Mr. Isidore Greenberger reorganized Bikur Cholim and gave my father the position of president.

The two worked together as colleagues and friends all the years that my father was in Boro Park, sharing many experiences together. Once again, Father put in his tireless efforts to create an organization that is a shining example of the *chesed*, loving-kindness, of *am Yisrael*. This included visiting the sick every Shabbos, arranging kosher food for Jewish patients in hospitals, and organizing sleeping accommodations for family members of hospitalized Jews. Bikur Cholim honored Father posthumously at their winter 2002/03 dinner along with several of its founding members.

The Iranian Youth

My father's last major project while still living in Boro Park was creating a committee to help the young Iranian immigrants escaping the dictatorial reign of Ayatollah Khomeini. One *erev Shabbos*, just before my mother lit candles, a woman walked into the house with a young man.

"Mrs. Rabinowicz," she said, "please, I need to speak to you. There are many young Jewish girls and boys here that escaped from Iran and have nowhere to live. Some of them literally sleep in the streets. I and another woman are trying to help these youths. This young man is one of them. Could you and Mr. Rabinowicz help us?"

"We would be happy to have you spend Shabbos with us," my mother told the youth. Turning to the woman, she said, "And right after Shabbos we will do something about helping these children."

She was as good as her word. That *motza'ei Shabbos* my father called together some of his friends for a meeting in his home. They formed a committee that night, immediately pledging money toward the cause and promising to get others involved. The new organization set up the Emergency Youth Fund in order to help these young people.

My mother served as secretary and did the bookkeeping for the project. She never wanted her name to appear as part of the committee. She said one Rabinowicz on the stationery was enough.

Some of these youths had been wealthy before leaving Iran, making their current situation that much more unbearable. The Iranian king, prior to Khomeini's rise to power, had a good relationship with the Jews, and many of them prospered under his rule. When Khomeini took control of the government, the Jews were persecuted.

One of the tasks the committee members undertook was to approach the local businesses they patronized to find jobs for these youths. Many of these young men and women were able to escape by coming to the United States as students. But as students they had no work permits and could not be hired legally. Additionally, since many of these children grew up in luxury, they found it hard to take jobs as menial workers, such as waitresses or cashiers. Many of the young men and women wanted to go to university and preferred studying to working. One boy told my parents about a cousin of his who was literally starving. She was the daughter of affluent parents and could not force herself to do the menial work that was offered her in her new country.

Because of the difficulty in finding work and also the difficulty in getting themselves to do the work, some of these youth were so poor they had nowhere to live; others lived in cheap basement apartments. Several of the committee members, including my parents, agreed to take Iranians into their own homes. It was not an easy thing to do, since not all of them were religious and not all of them were considerate to their host families.

My father and mother took in two teenage girls, who lived with them almost until my parents made aliyah to Eretz Yisrael. The girls surely missed home, and perhaps in their old lifestyle, they were used to spending money. Whatever the case, my mother discovered a hefty phone bill of several thousand dollars after the girls moved in. But as long as they could not fend for themselves my parents decided to keep them on. All in all, during the time that my parents worked on this project, the committee settled over forty young men and women with religious families.

His Love of Torah and Mitzvos

My father's love of learning was great, indeed, and it expressed itself in many ways. Not only did he push himself to learn as much as he could within the confines of his busy schedule, but in various ways he made sure to maintain a strong awareness of his spirituality. He literally loved the mitzvos and did whatever he had to in order to fulfill them.

Once he traveled to the Caribbean on a Monday morning and forgot his tefillin at home. My father did not panic, but he sounded agitated when he phoned my mother from the hotel after discovering his oversight.

She could sense that something was wrong. "Mechele, what is it? What's the matter?"

"I left my tefillin at home by mistake! Listen, early tomorrow morning go to the Pan Am desk at the airport and ship the tefillin to me, no matter what the cost. I'll pick them up at the airport. You can call Pan Am and find out what time the plane leaves. Be sure to get to the airport about two hours before departure."

"All right, whatever you say. I'll send the tefillin off to you tomorrow, no matter what the cost."

The next morning my mother rushed to the Pan Am building at the airport with the precious tefillin. The official she spoke to had to verify the contents of the package.

"What's in here, ma'am?"

"Phylacteries. It is a religious item with which one prays," my mother replied.

"Why are you sending this to the Caribbean?"

"My husband flew there for business, and he forgot them at home," my mother explained.

"Ma'am, I must open this package and see what they are exactly."

He proceeded to do so and looked at the tefillin suspiciously. He had never seen the likes of them before.

"Lady, I don't know what these are! I have to cut 'em open before I can allow them on board the plane."

Th official probably thought they were explosives or contraband.

"Oh no, sir. I can't allow you to do that! These are holy items used for prayer."

"Well, then, lady, they ain't goin' nowhere!"

My mother tried to get him to agree to send them without investigating further, but he would not give in. For lack of another option, she went home and telephoned my father. She told him all that had transpired. Understandably he was very upset.

The mitzvah of tefillin requires putting them on daily during the day. Since my father had no way of obtaining a pair in the Caribbean, he immediately took a plane back home. He suffered the monetary loss with no regrets.

Several hours later he appeared at home. "*Vie zenin de tefillin?* — Where are the tefillin?" he asked eagerly as he entered the house.

He managed to fulfill the mitzvah of tefillin since it was still day. Then he took his sacred bundle and flew back to the Caribbean to resume his business.

Chesed

My father expressed his love of doing *chesed* in many ways, aside from the various organizations and committees to which he gave of his time. It happened once, during the time he lived in London, that his brother-in-law Rav Shmuel Sperber became quite ill on Shabbos. He began spitting up blood, and my father went with him to the hospital that Shabbos. My aunt Miriam was terribly worried; she feared that he had contracted tuberculosis from her. How would she last out the long hours until the end of Shabbos to find out his condition?

Late Shabbos afternoon my father appeared at home. He was pale and exhausted from the three-hour walk. My mother rushed over to him, asking, "Mechele, why did you walk home on Shabbos? You look like you are collapsing!"

"I knew that Manitchka would be very worried about Shmuel. I wanted to let her know that he was feeling much better. He's going to be all right."

"Couldn't you wait till after Shabbos to let her know?" Mother queried.

"How could I do that when I knew that she was sick with worry! I had to let her know as soon as possible!"

In the year 1979, our cousin Avigayil Nadav, who lived in Tel Aviv with her husband Rav Yosef, was diagnosed with a brain tumor. She was mother to eleven children, none married at the time. Her youngest child was a mere baby. She needed immediate surgery, and the hospital of choice was New York University Hospital in Manhattan.

My father was the uncle who always gave a helping hand. Avigayil was admitted to the hospital, and Rav Yosef stayed at my parents' house for the next three months. My parents tried to give him strength and encouragement in whatever way possible.

Rav Daniel, Avigayil's younger brother, came, and he, too, stayed with my parents. Rav Daniel's help was vital, since Rav Yosef did not speak English. He went to the hospital daily with Rav Yosef and spoke to the doctors and took care of the financial matters for him. Rav Daniel stayed for about a month. When he returned to Eretz Yisrael, my mother took over by going regularly to the hospital.

After the initial surgery, the Nadavs returned to Eretz Yisrael. Sadly, the tumor continued growing, and it was necessary for Avigayil to have a second operation in 1980. Once again, they came to the United States.

Their oldest daughter, Shoshi, barely eighteen years old, was running the house. One day, when Avigayil was speaking to her on the phone, she expressed a desire to see her daughter. And so Shoshi joined her father at my parents' home. She stayed for three months. My father always tried to keep her spirits up. When Shoshi told him how worried she was that her mother was not speaking after her operation, he said, "It will be all right!" His faith in Hashem was strong, and his optimism heartened her.

He always made it a point to spend some time with Shoshi and ask about her day. This was a tremendous *chesed* for her. During the day she hardly spoke a word to anyone, and sometimes she would barely see a living soul. Avigayil wasn't talking after her surgery, and there was a black woman in a vegetative state in the other bed, so there was practically no one for Shoshi to talk to all day. My father realized this and was there for Shoshi, as busy as he was.

One thing that both Shoshi and her father remarked upon was that they never saw my father without his hat and jacket. Never once in the months that they lived in our house did they see him in his shirtsleeves. Father always felt he was in the presence of Hashem and conducted himself as one would in front of a king.

Rav Yosef Nadav spent six months at my parents' during the two visits in this trying period in his life. In later years, when he was living in Eretz Yisrael, my father visited Avigayil in Tel Aviv, even though he wasn't well and walking was becoming more and more difficult. He took a taxi from Yerushalayim, a costly venture, since traveling via public transportation was too difficult for him.

After Avigayil passed away, the Nadav children continued to remain very close to my parents. They would often visit their favorite great-aunt and -uncle, bringing their new wives or husbands and children.

When I was nearly sixteen years old, my parents decided

to spend the summer in New Hampshire. Our destination was Bethlehem, which boasted a kosher hotel with a daily minyan. The air in this most beautiful and scenic area is pollen-free, and many religious Jewish allergy sufferers would come to spend their summers there. We rented a bungalow near the hotel.

That summer Mime Perele and Fetter Reb Moishele were going away, and their son Boruch was staying behind in the city. As soon as my father heard, he invited his nephew to come with us.

Every day, first thing in the morning, my father learned with the two Boruchs, his son and his nephew, the *sefer Reishis Chochmah*, a *mussar sefer* written about four hundred years ago. Learning this *sefer* is a *segulah* for *yiras Shamayim*, a merit for attaining the fear of Heaven. Not only did our cousin enjoy being and learning with his uncle, but he described the feeling of warmth and caring he received. Mime Perele always said that Fetter Mechele treated her Boruch like his own son.

Torah Study

Because he was a businessman, many people called my father "Mr. Rabinowicz," and some of his business associates even called him "Mike" — he always shunned the title of rabbi. But in his soul he was a true *ben Torah*, and he possessed the essence of an *Admor*, a chassidic Rebbe.

Despite the heavy financial burdens he carried upon his shoulders for many years, the many projects he completed successfully for the Jewish community, and the varied areas of Torah learning he delved in, my father managed to finish

Shas five times during his lifetime.

When my father made his last — his fifth — *siyum haShas*, he was filled with joy. He had been suffering from kidney stones for a while and had not been able to learn as usual. Once he recuperated he was able to finish *Shas*. The *siyum* was held at the Sefardishe shul. That celebration stands out in the minds of many people. It was obvious how joyful he was to accomplish, once again, that which was so dear to his heart.

Once, when his brother Reb Yisroel was sick, my father made an oath to finish the entire *Shas* in three years. This was quite an undertaking. If one were to learn one *daf* a day, it would take seven years to finish *Shas*. He would have to do it in less than half the time. During the day he was busy with his business and various community affairs, and inevitably he got behind in his learning schedule. When he was in the third year of his *neder* and thought he would not meet his deadline, he would sit and learn nonstop, sometimes around the clock.

When my father started the smelting business with two other partners, it was his job to take care of the day-to-day running of the enterprise. But he was spending so much time learning that the partners became extremely annoyed at him. "What kind of partner is this who sits and learns all day? There is no one taking care of the business!" they said. They dissolved the partnership, and my father was left to start a new business on his own. But he had no choice. If he had made an oath to finish *Shas* in three years, then that was what he was going to do and nothing would get in his way.

Not only would my father fulfill his own requirements for learning Torah, but he made sure to fulfill the commandment to teach Torah to others. For most of his life he gave *shiurim* in various Torah subjects, sometimes to *rabbanim* and *talmidei chachamim*, Torah scholars, and sometimes to *ba'alei batim*, businessmen.

He gave a *shiur* in his home in Boro Park for many years as well as in the Congregation Anshei Sefard, the shul to which he belonged. The main part of the *shiur* my father gave at home was learning through the *Sefer HaMitzvos* of the Rambam. He felt that learning the *Sefer HaMitzvos* was most important for a Jew. He once told his grandnephew Avraham Nadav that it was hard for a Jew to learn all of the Torah. A good way to gain knowledge of the Torah was by learning the Rambam's *Sefer HaMitzvos*. If one wanted to know Torah thoroughly, it was worth his while to learn this *sefer*.

Rav Yosef Nadav, the Sperbers' son-in-law, stayed with my parents for six months when his wife had surgery in New York University Hospital. Sometimes he attended my father's Shabbos *shiurim*. He was very impressed with them and told my father that he must write them down. My father replied that during the week he never had time, and on Shabbos he couldn't write. After Shabbos he did not have time to do so either, since there was always something important waiting for him the minute Shabbos was out. The only notes he had were some thoughts he jotted down on small scraps of paper to use while presenting the *shiur*. For the duration of the time that Rav Nadav was a guest in my parents' home, he would write down the synopsis of the *shiur* after Shabbos whenever he attended.

During Father's retirement years in Bayit Vegan, my mother persuaded him to put together his *shiurim* in book form. He engaged a writer, one of the editors of the *Hamodia* newspaper, to transcribe his insights, written on the small scraps of paper and from the notes written by Rav Nadav. The result was his sefer *Zimras HaAretz* (Song of the Land).

My father learned Kabbalah, although he didn't talk about it. Once someone asked my father if he could look up something in the *Zohar*. He became extremely angry, saying, "Do you know who wrote the *Zohar*? Do you know what kind of person he was? You don't just 'look into the *Zohar*'! You need to be on the level to do so." My mother said that she had rarely seen him so angry. But it upset him exceedingly that people took learning Kabbalah lightly.

There were certain *sefarim* my father learned that meant a lot to him. One of these was a small Kabbalah *sefer* that he took with him on his travels. He once forgot it on the airplane. As soon as he realized his loss, he called up the airline and explained his plight. They said that the plane he had traveled on had already been cleaned, and all articles left behind on planes were dumped together in one large container. It would be impossible to find his one little item.

He was determined to find his *sefer*, and he offered to pay the airport officials whatever they asked of him in order to do so. He insisted on coming down to the storage area of the airport himself, and he sifted through the gigantic crate of items. He was unrelenting until he found his precious *sefer*.

A cousin of mine recalled that in May 1979 my father approached him with a request.

"David,* I know you are a good and serious learner. Lately my eyes have been giving me a lot of trouble, and it is affecting my learning. I am not able to learn as much as I used to. I want to make a business deal with you."

"Yes, Fetter Mechele. What can I do for you?"

"I want to pay you for one hour of your learning every day, and the merit of your learning should go into my account in Heaven."

My cousin expressed his amazement over the fact that my father would not agree to a lessening of his merit for learning, even in a situation where he had no control. This was so important to my father that if he were able he would pay for that incredible merit.

I found another contract written in the same year stipulating that Father would pay another young scholar $150 a month for the merit of his learning one hour a day. In the year 1979 my father was paying at least two people a monthly stipend of several hundred dollars for the merit of their learning one hour a day for his sake!

My father also made a contract between himself and Rabbi Shlomo Weiner. It was witnessed by my husband, Yechezkel Toporowitch. It showed my father's great love of Torah and his belief in the great merit Torah learning bestows upon an individual.

The agreement stipulated that after my father's 120 years upon this earth Rabbi Weiner would learn for ten years for the elevation of my father's soul. The first year he would learn a certain amount of Mishnah and light two candles every day for his soul. The next nine years he would learn Gemara and *Rishonim* for a full hour every day. As payment he would receive three hundred dollars each month. The contract was never put into effect, probably due to lack of funds.

How many people would think along these lines during his lifetime?

Father's Approach to Money

My father's idea of *tzedakah* was not typical of the average observant Jew. He was never a very wealthy man, yet he was a tremendous *ba'al tzedakah*. He gave money when he had it, and he gave when he did not have it.

He supported his sisters Malkele and Telchele for the duration of their lives, as well as other members of the family. He was very close to his sister Perele, and he worried about her welfare. He often sent substantial checks to Fetter Moishele. In their home one could often hear, "Mechel sent a check. We have to call him up to thank him."

"Once my parents wanted to go away for the summer," my cousin Reb Shmelke told me. "Fetter Mechele asked my mother, 'Perele, why don't you go away?' She answered, 'Not always does one have money to go away.' He asked her how much it would cost, and she gave him a figure. He said that he would send her the money and that she must go. And that's exactly what he did."

One summer Father and Mother planned to visit Yechezkel and me in Eretz Yisrael. When Perele Leifer, the Chuster Rebbetzin, heard that her brother was going away, she cried inconsolably. She had a heart condition and was not feeling well at the time. My father paid for her to go on vacation. She stayed in a hotel for a little while but then returned home. Not long after that, she was taken to the hospital, and within a matter of days passed away. My aunt was buried in Eretz Yisrael, and my father sat *shivah* in our home in Bnei Brak.

It was sad to see my father sitting alone with his memories of grief. He told me how his sister and the older children were saved by the righteous gentile Raoul Wallenberg and spent the end of the war in a Red Cross camp. My uncle had been deported to one of the concentration camps during the war but survived the ordeal. After the war, my aunt and uncle were reunited. They emigrated to the United States, living in several locales before ending up in Boro Park. Today their oldest son Reb Shmuel (Shmelke) serves as the Chuster Rebbe in Boro Park, and their second son, Reb Boruch Pinchas, serves in that capacity in Eretz Yisrael.

My mother's uncle Fetter Leibenu, the Trisker Rebbe, was a great *ba'al chesed* during the war years in London. But he had no means of income, and my father helped him out financially while he lived in London. Later the Rebbe moved to Bnei Brak. He was quite old at that time, but he had a *beis midrash* on Rabbi Tarfon Street and built up a following. It seems that my father continued to support him at this stage of his life as well. The Rebbe was old and sick when he wrote the letter that I found. It is undated, but apparently it was written at the time my father was going through financial difficulties, perhaps during the bankruptcy. The Trisker Rebbe's letter demonstrates my father's generosity at any time, no matter what was going on in his life.

Malka Weiss, wife of Rabbi Yaakov Weiss, who was instrumental in getting my father involved in Ohel, told us that she often saw my father walking on the streets of Boro Park and, in later years, of Bayit Vegan. She remembered many times seeing him suddenly cross over to the other side of the street. She realized that the reason he did so was because he would see someone approaching to whom he had given a loan and was unable to repay it. My father would cross the street because he didn't want the recipient of the loan to be embarrassed upon coming face to face with him and being reminded that he couldn't repay the debt he owed him.

But my father did not assist only family and friends. My father would help anyone, relative or stranger.

Mrs. Berger* came from Israel to the United States for medical reasons. Since she was a foreigner, she had no Medicaid or other medical insurance. Her medical condition required that she take a certain expensive medication, and therefore she was constantly in need of funds. My aunt called her up once to ask her if she needed to buy more medicine. The woman said she had bought it already. She said that there was a man who lived on 47th Street, a Mr. Rabinowicz, who had given her husband four hundred dollars and pledged this amount for the next several months. And this, despite the fact that to Father she was a perfect stranger.

His love of *tzedakah* was such that in 1986 my father established a trust, The M & M Charity Fund (using the initials of his and my mother's names). The purpose of the trust was to distribute funds for religious, charitable, and educational purposes and to give grants and interest-free loans for *tzedakah* purposes.

Each night my mother would go through the mail, opening the letters with her letter opener. There would be piles of *tzedakah* envelopes, both from institutions and from private people.

"Mechele," she'd ask my father, "what shall I do with all these *tzedakah* envelopes?"

"Don't throw out even one! Answer them all!" He didn't even look to see from where they came!

And so she would write checks, one after the other, for each envelope. When Shoshi Nadav came to live in my parents' home for several months, she was very surprised to see my mother writing out so many checks. My mother said that my father had told her to answer each letter. She told Shoshi that their financial situation was not so good anymore, and they could no longer afford to be so generous, but my father did not want to hear of it. He wanted to give to everyone just as he always had.

At the celebration of his fifth *siyum haShas*, this aspect of his character was amply demonstrated. At such a time, the host could expect to be given gifts from his guests. Instead, he handed out checks! "I don't take checks. I give checks," he announced. "I did not invite you in order to receive presents."

Who didn't know my father? Everyone came to him for help. He helped the Ponevezher Rav, Rav Yosef Chaim Kahaneman, collect money during his stay in America. The *rav* was planning to build a yeshivah in Bnei Brak. When my father was in Eretz Yisrael, he went to see how the construction was going. The Ponevezher Rav kissed him and said, "You see what you have helped us build!" Once the yeshivah was built, the *rav* brought over a beautiful, antique *aron kodesh* from Italy. One of the things that attract tourists to the yeshivah is this very special *aron kodesh*.

I found many letters of appreciation from various institutions commending my father for his generosity. There were numerous letters from Lakewood thanking him for his support of the yeshivah. Besides the form letters sent by the executive office, he received personal letters from the *rosh yeshivah*, HaRav Shneur Kotler, *zt"l*. Rav Kotler wrote in one of these letters that my father's support was an expression of his deep love of Torah and her scholars.

Not only did my father support the Lakewood Yeshivah

financially, but his love of Torah made him go out of his way to help Rav Kotler and his mother in other ways. The *rebbetzin* survived her husband, the great Rav Aharon Kotler, *zt"l,* by many years. She lived in Boro Park, a block away from my parents' home. Sometimes, when my father was driving, he would see the *rebbetzin* walking, and he would give her a lift. He told the *rebbetzin* that if she ever needed to go somewhere she should call him, and if he was available he would take her happily.

The Skverer Rebbe wanted my father's help in the creation of the town of New Square. My father and my brother, Boruch, were given a tour of the grounds of the proposed town by the Rebbe. He begged my father to plan the town. My father told him that he was not an architect and declined the job because he refused to use his profession for *tzedakah* and public projects. He wanted to fulfill the words of the Torah, "*V'hiyisem nekiyim* — And you shall be clean." His experience with the Boro Park mikveh taught him that although he did the job totally for the sake of the mitzvah, inevitably there would be some people who would claim that he had his own interests in mind and suspect him of making a profit from it.

Perhaps as a result of this interaction, when one of my father's prospective *mechutanim,* Boruch's future father-in-law, Mr. Feldman, asked the Skverer Rebbe for information about my father, the Rebbe had only praise for him.

To my father money was to be used for the sake of Heaven. Money was given to a person to use for Hashem's mitzvos. A monetary loss simply meant that Hashem didn't want him to have this money at this point in his life, and therefore a loss never bothered him. His reaction to losing money was to give even more *tzedakah* than before.

One winter a pipe burst in the basement, where my father had his office and storage room for his export business, due to the extreme cold. The basement flooded, the water level rising by the minute. Many of the electrical appliances that my father kept in the storage room to be exported to the Caribbean — washing machines, ovens, small refrigerators, electric tools — were ruined. His papers and catalogues were soaked, floating in the rising water.

Everyone spent the whole night bailing water. They worked for hours in the nearly knee-deep, icy water. They were all in a foul mood — all except Father. He kept smiling as if nothing had happened, singing cheerfully the whole time!

This was my father's attitude in the face of monetary loss. He wanted to let the others know that they should not be upset about what had happened. He was certain that everything would turn out for the best.

Another time my father was walking in the street on Shabbos. *Oy, oy, oy!* he thought to himself. *I forgot to take my watch off at home*. Some people wear a fancy watch on Shabbos outside the house as well as at home, considering it a piece of jewelry and therefore exempt from the prohibition of carrying on Shabbos. My father, however, did not. Had he not stopped at some point in his walk, he would have been able to walk straight home wearing the watch. But since he had stopped, he was no longer able to continue walking.

"I'll leave it here under the tree. I'll come back on *motza'ei Shabbos* to get it."

It was a gold watch, worth five hundred dollars.

After Shabbos, on the way home from shul, he looked for

it under the tree, but it was no longer there. He searched the local Jewish papers for an announcement that a gold watch had been found but to no avail.

Gam zu l'tovah, he thought. *This too, is for the good. Hashem wanted me to lose some money now. Very good! I am happy that nothing worse happened to me. It's only money after all!*

He did not have a moment's distress over losing it. He related this story to Shoshi Nadav, adding that one should never be upset about losing money. It was merely something Hashem gave to you to use as He saw fit. That was the amazing quality we saw in him. You can't fake that!

Shabbos

My father was an extremely busy man. He wasn't home much, being so involved with his businesses and the affairs of the community. On *erev Shabbos* he often came home late. But he had his special rituals in preparing for Shabbos.

I remember that he always cut his nails on Friday. He would do this in his study, wrapping the nails carefully in a piece of newspaper, making sure none were left out or had fallen on the floor. Then he would store the little package in the top left desk drawer. The *minhag* in his family was to burn nails. My father kept the nails until *erev Pesach* morning when he performed the mitzvah of *biur chametz.* It was fascinating for me to see him gather fifty small parcels of his cut nails and take them outside, together with the little parcels of *chametz* he had gathered the night before during *bedikas chametz,* and throw them into the bonfire the neighborhood boys had lit for the purpose of burning the *chametz.*

He went to the mikveh before Shabbos, as did many Jews, chassidic or not. My father also went to the mikveh every morning before davening *shacharis*. This was so important to him that he went even when he was older and it was hard for him to walk.

Shabbos was special for us in many ways since we didn't see Father much during the week. As children, we enjoyed the singing of *zemiros* at the Shabbos table. My father would sing each and every one that was found in the siddur. To him Shabbos would have felt incomplete if he had missed out on even one. Much later on in his life, when he was critically ill, we realized how important his *zemiros* were to him. His singing would bond him to Hashem in the midst of his pain and suffering, serving as a source of comfort.

An interesting feature of Father's singing was his enthusiasm and the way he clapped his hands. According to the halachah, on Shabbos one should clap his hands with a *shinui*, a change, doing it differently than during the week. The reason for this is that when one claps to the rhythm of the music one might forget that it is Shabbos and inadvertently bang on a musical instrument. My father wanted to give Shabbos his full respect and enthusiasm. So during the week, when he sang, he'd clap his hands differently from the usual way, clapping the back of one hand against the palm of the other. On Shabbos, therefore, he was able to clap both palms together, a *shinui* from what he did during the week, and express his joy fully and loudly.

My father had an interesting way of interacting with us at the Shabbos table. Besides asking us what we had learned in school during that week, he had his own unique set of questions for us. He would ask each one of the four siblings three questions, each set of questions matching the age level of the child. There was a *Torah fraga,* a Torah question, a *mitzvah fraga,* and an *algemeina veltlecha fraga,* a general knowledge question. He gave us a nickel after Shabbos for each question we answered correctly. In order to get us really enthusiastic about our questions, he gave us an extra nickel if we wrote them down in a special notebook after Shabbos. I remember vividly how one of the first things I did after Shabbos was to write my questions down in my notebook so that I could get the extra nickel.

Sometimes on Shabbos my father would challenge us with a really difficult question. He would present it to all of us, and whoever got the answer would get the enormous sum of a dollar or even two. One of these "super" questions might be, "Who was So-and-so mentioned in the Torah?" — a name that meant nothing to us. The answer might be found somewhere in a *Rashi.*

What I think is so interesting about this interaction with us is that he made an effort to stimulate us at our level. He was a very deep thinker and a holy person. Yet he had patience for us and was not above coming down to our level. On Shabbos, when he had extra time to spend with us, he used the opportunity to create a connection and to have fun with us.

After the Friday night meal, Father stayed up to read the parashah out loud with the *trop,* that particular way of sounding the words when reading the Torah in shul. No matter how late it was and how tired he was, he would always read through the parashah.

Sometimes I stayed up to listen. I thought if I listened long enough I would also learn to read the Torah with the *trop*. I never managed to get it right but would imitate some of the sounds, especially the *shalsheles*, a tone that repeats three times.

During the winter my father gave a Shabbos *shiur* for *ba'alei batim* (working men) on the parashah on Friday night after the meal. During the summer he gave his *shiur* at *seudah shelishis*, the afternoon Shabbos meal, at our dining-room table. He was very happy and excited about this *shiur*. In later years, when he had his export business and finished our basement, he gave the *shiur* downstairs. As children, we always felt happy and excited to put out the beer, soda, and peanuts in preparation. It made us feel important to help our father with his *shiur*.

Havdalah had its unique flavor and a special *niggun*. When he made the *berachah* on the fire, *borei me'orei ha'eish*, he'd look at his nails under the light of the flame and then pass his fingers through the fire several times. After drinking the wine, he put out the flame of the Havdalah candle by spilling some of the leftover wine. He then wet his fingers with the wine and wrote the Hebrew letters *shin*, *dalet*, and *yud* (the name of Hashem read as "*Shakai*") on his forehead and circle the letters. He would say certain words to himself that we could not hear. Then he would wet his fingers again with the wine and put them into his *bekeshe* and pants pockets, a *segulah* for filling them with money. He wet his fingers a third time and put the wine to his nostrils, smelling it. I never found out what that was a *segulah* for.

My father never skipped *melaveh malkah*, no matter what was going on or how tired he was. He lit two candles for the elevation of the soul of David HaMelech, murmuring the appropriate prayers all the while. He always washed his hands for challah and ate something else, and then he sang all of the *motza'ei Shabbos* and *melaveh malkah zemiros*. He would do all this whether or not he was alone at the table. We ate something only if we were hungry; otherwise we passed up *melaveh malkah*. But for my father it was not a matter of being hungry. For him it was as important as any one of the Shabbos meals.

Rosh Chodesh

Nothing outstanding went on in our home on Rosh Chodesh, the day of the new moon. But there is a commandment that Jews bless the moon, to recite *kiddush levanah*, during the time between the new moon and the full moon. The congregation goes outside after *ma'ariv* and, upon sighting the moon, says a particular prayer.

It may happen sometimes that due to inclement weather the moon is covered by clouds and cannot be seen. One month this was exactly the case. Night after night my father went out and looked up at the night sky, hoping that the moon would break through the clouds, but it never did. The last opportunity for blessing the moon had arrived, and my father had still been unable to do so.

He did not give up on his mitzvos so easily. He came home very late that night.

"Where were you until such a late hour?" my mother asked him anxiously when he finally walked through the door.

"I've been trying to say *kiddush levanah* for the past two weeks and could not see the moon because of the terrible weather we are having. Since tonight was the last chance, I decided to rent a helicopter and look for the moon."

My mother was not terribly surprised. This was exactly the type of thing he would do in such a situation.

"So what happened?"

"It took me a while to find out where the helicopter field is. But after I got there, I did not have to wait long to hire a pilot to take me up. We circled around for about an hour till we found the moon. I was so happy that my trip was not in vain that I spent some extra time davening and saying *tehillim*."

"How much did it cost?" my mother wanted to know.

He told her. It would have been considered a lot of money for a pleasure trip, but for my father no amount was too much to spend on a mitzvah.

Yamim Tovim

The Rosh HaShanah and Yom Kippur holidays were very special because Father was always the chazzan for *shacharis*. My father davened *shacharis* for the congregation on Yom Kippur, as he did on Rosh HaShanah, even after he moved to Eretz Yisrael. When he was older, the doctor forbade him to fast due to his eye condition. In addition, he had other conditions that caused weakness and dizziness. But naturally none of this stopped him from fasting, despite the fact that he was on his feet a good part of the day as a *ba'al tefillah*. His unflinching determination enabled him to carry out these incredible acts of strength.

He continued to be a *ba'al tefillah* until a year and a half before he passed away. This was an amazing feat; he was very weak and could no longer see well enough to read. But age did stop him eventually. At the age of eighty-two he davened for the congregation for the last time while sitting down, saying the whole *tefillah* by heart. The following year the shul sent a committee of people asking him to please let someone younger take over the role of *ba'al tefillah,* and he had no choice but to give up this beloved mitzvah. And so, it was just that one last Rosh HaShanah of his life that he davened privately, without carrying the congregation along with him in his intense service to Hashem.

There was an interesting custom performed at home on *erev Yom Kippur.* Before the *seudah mafsekes,* the last meal before the fast, my father was served a plate of sponge cake, called "*lekach.*" *Lekach* in Hebrew means a lesson or a teaching. We would stand on line, and, one by one, he would tell each of us, "*Beit lekach* — Ask for sponge cake." We would reply, "*Ich beit lekach* — I want *lekach.*" He would give us two pieces, and at the same time would give us many good wishes for the new year. Then he would say to us, "*Ich beit lekach tzurik* — I want some *lekach* back," and we would return one of the pieces to him while wishing him a good year.

As a child, I never knew the source of this custom, although I enjoyed the delicious sponge cake. Recently I discovered what it is. If there is a decree in Heaven upon a person that he must ask others for food as a beggar does, he can, so to speak, live out the decree by asking for food on *erev Yom Kippur.* Both our grandfather and uncle, the first and second Skolyer Rebbes, performed this custom.

We built our sukkah in the driveway next to the house. For *sechach* we used the branches of pine trees. I still remember the pungent odor of the pine needles and the pattern of the green flowered print material we used to cover the wooden walls. Often it rained, and my father would sit in the dining room waiting for it to stop.

My daughter Rochy remembers visiting her grandparents on Sukkos. Her *zeidy* sent the children outside every few minutes to see just how much it was raining and if it was letting up. Eventually there would be a lull in the rainfall. We would quickly rush out to the sukkah, make Kiddush, and wash and eat a *kezayis* (a measurement the size of a small egg) of challah. Once we did that, Father would relax, knowing that he had fulfilled the commandment to eat his meal in the sukkah.

Hoshana Rabbah was a day of prayer and reverence. At night my father stayed up until he finished the *tikun*, the special prayers said on that night, at about three or four in the morning. Then he came home and went to sleep.

On Simchas Torah my father was always given the great honor of *chasan Bereishis* in shul. And so, every Simchas Torah my father invited the whole congregation home for Kiddush. My father invited his *shiur* attendees, friends, and relatives to join us. At this occasion, he had a most interesting way of giving a Torah discourse. It was something he'd learned in his father's home, although his father said *divrei Torah* in this manner often and my father did so only once a year.

He would choose two people, one to open a *Chumash* of his choice to a random page and read the *pasuk* at the top of the page and the other to do the same with a Gemara. My father would take a moment to think and then proceeded to give a discourse that connected the two passages.

Sometimes he spoke for more than an hour. It was a most amazing feat, since he could not prepare in advance, and it required a tremendous command of *Shas*. He never got stuck as far as I could tell.

At the end of his Torah discourse, the men moved over the tables, and they sang and danced around the room until it was time for *ma'ariv*. When they davened *ma'ariv* together, we knew that this *yom tov* was over until the next year.

My father's Chanukah lighting was special, too. After igniting the wicks floating in olive oil and singing *HaNeiros Hallalu*, he sang *Ana B'Ko'ach*, the *tefillah* of Rabbi Nechunya ben HaKanah. It is written that one should say this *mizmor* with a sweet voice, and one should be careful to concentrate on the words because of the holiness they contain. My father sang each word seven times: "*Ana, ana, ana, ana, ana, ana, ana, b'ko'ach, b'ko'ach, b'ko'ach, b'ko'ach, b'ko'ach, b'ko'ach, b'ko'ach...*" with a very special and haunting melody passed down through the generations from the holy Ba'al Shem Tov. It was hypnotic listening to him go through the whole thing.

As young children we didn't have much patience for such long ceremonies, but later in life I appreciated it much more. He sang the *Ana B'Koach* with his eyes closed and with intensity and depth of feeling, so that he seemed to be going into the higher spheres with each word he uttered.

We played a card game, *kreindelach*, on Chanukah with my father instead of the traditional dreidel. He probably played this game with his family when he was a child. He made the cards from pieces of cardboard the shirts came back with from the dry cleaner. Playing *kreindelach* with my father brings such fond memories that I always try to make time to play the game with my children and grandchildren.

Purim was a happy time. Many people came to the house collecting *tzedakah*, and my father gave generously. I don't recall that my father ever got drunk, though. My mother never bought us Purim costumes, but made them herself. It was more fun that way.

Father tried to make Purim enjoyable for us kids. He would sit at the table, writing up a play, his own original story, and then he gave each child a part and acted out the story together with them. He did this purely for family fun. His humor and ability to have fun with us was a big feature of his personality.

Pesach was a time of hard work for everyone, including my father. He baked his own matzos, a very expensive product in light of the fact that he had to rent the matzah factory for the duration of the time it took him to finish baking the amount of matzos he needed, working with a limited number of people. In the dining room, my father would prepare many packages of matzos to give to others who could not afford them.

Pesach itself stands out in my mind as very special. Curling up on the couch next to my father in his white *kittel* when we got tired is one of my fondest memories. How he managed to carry on late into the night with such energy is beyond me, since he worked so hard during the week. His love of mitzvos just kept him going.

The most amazing aspect of the Pesach seder was when my father fulfilled the mitzvah of eating the *marror*, the bitter herbs. He understood this commandment to mean that we should feel, to some degree, the bitterness of being slaves in a foreign land. To that end, he performed the mitzvah to eat bitter herbs in a way that literally tortured him. He took a solid piece of horseradish the size of a *kezayis*. He recited the *berachah* out loud and then bit into it and chewed it slowly until he finished the whole thing.

Many people cannot eat the horseradish on seder night

even if it had been ground up an hour or two earlier. But what my father was doing was biting into the hot root itself and slowly chewing it until it was finely ground up in his mouth. His mouth and nose burned as though they were on fire, and we watched in fascination as the tears rolled down his cheeks. He opened his mouth from time to time to breathe in cool air and occasionally rest in the middle of his ordeal.

He never spoke a word until he finished eating. It looked like absolute torture to us, and we had no idea how he could force himself to do it. My father's stomach became upset easily, and there were many foods he never ate because of it (Shabbos cholent, for example). The doctor had told him that it was very damaging to his stomach and intestines to eat horseradish in such a manner. But my father was adamant. He always said you can't get hurt from doing a mitzvah. One thing he had learned, though, was to chew the horseradish until it was finely ground up. If ever he swallowed a piece, even a tiny one, his stomach would burn for days after. Whoever spent a Pesach seder with us remembers vividly the spectacle of my father's superhuman feat.

The best fun we had seder night was when we had Mr. Cooper* as a guest. Although no longer young, he still worked as a traveling salesman. He was a widower and came to us quite often for the seder. My father placed Mr. Cooper next to him on the couch, that very special place of honor. They both had pillows behind their backs so that they could recline comfortably like kings.

As the seder progressed late into the night, Mr. Cooper would doze off. One of us children would creep up silently behind him, pull out one of the feathers from the pillow, and tickle him behind the ears until he woke with a start. By the time he came to full consciousness and opened his eyes, the culprit would be back in his or her seat reading the Haggadah with intense concentration, while the rest of us stifled our giggles. The poor man had no idea what that queer sensation had been that roused him, and soon he would be nodding off again. It wouldn't be long before one of us was at it again until Mother or Father stopped us.

Although we had good fun at his expense, we were always nice to Mr. Cooper and talked to him about his travels. He must have had relatives, but he preferred making the seder with us.

My father would not let us steal the *afikoman.* He put it inside the front of his *kittel* in order to protect it from our seeking hands. This was a *minhag,* a custom, based on the words in *parashas Shemos, "misharosam tzeruros b'simlosam* — their food bundles in their clothes." Sometimes I tried to get the *afikoman* out of Father's *kittel* when I thought he was nodding off for a few moments, but he was too alert for me. Of course, he didn't want to disappoint us and always asked each one of us what we wanted for *afikoman* even though he never had to bargain with us to get it back. We always got what we asked for, even when we were his guests as married children.

On one occasion that elusive prize, the *afikoman,* was actually stolen. Boruch's daughter Chani was the culprit.

"At the Pesach seder, when I was eleven years old, I decided to steal the *afikoman* from Zeidy. I got up to help Bubby serve, since we were up to *Shulchan Oreich.* When I put down the bowl of soup in front of Zeidy, he had just pulled a handkerchief out of his pocket, and the *afikoman* was in easy reach. I leaned over and took it. He was totally shocked, and so was everyone else. Bubby came into the dining room and said that she couldn't believe I'd stolen it. She said it had been years and years since anyone had done so, since Zeidy never let. My father explained that since Zeidy grew up in a house where miracles occurred, he used to say, 'If I let someone steal the *afikoman,* maybe they will ask me to do a miracle for them.' He was lucky, because I only asked for a camera."

No matter how late it was or how tired my father was he sang all the songs of *Nirtzah* patiently and with relish, right up to the end. He never left out a single one. My parents were quite elderly when Boruch and his family decided to spend a Pesach with them in Bayit Vegan. It must have been very late when the Shabbos clock turned off the lights, and they had not yet finished the seder. My father continued singing the songs of the Haggadah by heart. Chavi's son, Yisrael, was tired and wanted to finish quickly, so he tried to skip over some of the paragraphs but was unsuccessful. His grandfather knew the exact text of the Haggadah and insisted on saying all of it. When it came to doing a mitzvah, Father did not know how to compromise.

As on Simchas Torah, my father held a *simchas yom tov* on the last day of Pesach, which he called a *"seudas Ba'al Shem Tov."* He printed formal invitations for these *yom tov* get-togethers (he held one on Shavuos, too). He would not only say *divrei Torah* at this *seudas Besht,* but he would also tell stories from the life of the Ba'al Shem Tov. The spread was a little more fancy than for the weekly Shabbos *shiur,* and we children loved to help set it up. There was always a lot of singing, which went on for hours. Father's true essence of a Rebbe really came to the fore on these occasions.

Eretz Yisrael

On one of her trips to Eretz Yisrael, years before they made aliyah, my mother found out that one of her relatives, a distant Twersky cousin, was a member of the *chevrah kaddisha* in charge of selling plots on Har HaZeisim. She decided to contact this relative about purchasing two plots. Mother acquired two adjacent plots in Chelkas Volin, to be paid out in installments.

When she returned home, she told my father what she had done. He was surprised but realized that it was a good plan. It says that when one purchases a *kever,* a grave site, it ensures long life.

My father and mother loved the land of our heritage, Eretz Yisrael. Mother visited often, about once a year, since all of her siblings lived there. My father also made the trip, sometimes with my mother and sometimes alone. Their dream was to move to Yerushalayim.

Father's love for Eretz Yisrael and for the *kedushah* of the Holy Land was apparent in many ways. In the days before the recapture of the Old City and the Kosel, my father was visiting a *rosh yeshivah* he was friendly with who lived near East Jerusalem. The *rosh yeshivah* informed my father that there was a house nearby from whose roof one could catch sight of the Kosel. My father promptly asked to be taken there, and he made the climb up several flights of steps so he could get a glimpse of the holy Western Wall.

After the Six-Day War, when the Israeli army reclaimed the Old City of Yerushalayim, my father decided to come for a very short trip just so he could daven at the Kosel and other holy sites. He would fly in, take a taxi to Yerushalayim, daven at the Kosel, continue with the taxi to Kever Rachel, then to Me'aras HaMachpeilah in Chevron, and return to the airport for the flight back home.

That is exactly what he did. But the plane he took to Eretz Yisrael suffered mechanical difficulties on the way and was forced to stop off in Rome. My father didn't go to a hotel to rest because he didn't know when the flight would continue on its way, so he waited in the airport until the plane was repaired. The entire flight there took twenty-five hours. Despite it all, he carried out his itinerary as he had planned, taking the taxi from stop to stop with no rests in between. He had no more time than that to spend, and it was important to him to make the trip for those few hours of intense prayer even under those very difficult conditions.

One summer he spent Tishah B'Av at the Kosel. The heat must have been unbearable and the thirst intolerable, but davening and saying *tehillim* at the Kosel was so important to him that he did not let the discomforts get in the way. On another occasion, he stayed at the home of Rav Beinish Finkel, the Mirrer *rosh yeshivah,* for Yom Kippur so that he could spend the day davening at the Kosel.

In the summer of 1984, my father and mother actualized their dream of making aliyah to Eretz Yisrael. Had it been up to my mother, they would have made the move years earlier. Her sisters, Chaya and Miriam, and her brother, Yossik, all lived in Eretz Yisrael. (Polly had passed away several years earlier.) Father's family lived in New York, and he did not want to leave them. But on *erev Rosh HaShanah* 5731 (1971) tragedy occurred.

My father was very close to his brother Reb Yisroel and loved him deeply. He claimed that his brother was a *malach,* an angel. Reb Yisroel had no children of his own, and he took very special care of his invalid wife. But he never complained, and his face always shone with joy. My father always wanted to do whatever he could for his brother. Perhaps that is why Father made a *neder* to learn the entire *Shas* in three years in Reb Yisroel's merit when he was sick.

My uncle had been a chassidic Rebbe for most of his life, having had congregations in Romania, London, New York, Miami Beach, and now in Tel Aviv. When the apartment was purchased for him, all the neighbors but one signed an agreement to his having a synagogue in the building. My father was very concerned that his brother have a shul in his house. On his trips to Eretz Yisrael, my father did whatever he could to see that things worked out for Reb Yisroel, making sure that he had a regular minyan.

A year and a half after my aunt and uncle moved in, the neighbor who had never given his permission for the shul started making trouble. He incited the other neighbors to protest, and before long the Municipality sent my uncle an order to close down the shul. When he refused to comply, some neighbors called the police on Shabbos. The minyan-goers were dispersed, and Reb Yisroel was left without a congregation. Within the next few days he developed a fever and a severe infection. He was taken to the hospital and put on antibiotics. At first he improved, but just before Rosh HaShanah he took a turn for the worse.

On *erev Rosh HaShanah,* he passed away. The doctors could not explain why, since medically it should not have happened. But we all knew that our wonderful Fetter Reb S'rulche had died of a broken heart!

When my uncle became ill, Father had booked a flight to Israel for right after Rosh HaShanah. But now it was too late. He was incredulous at the turn of events, at the tragedy of his brother's death, and broke out in uncontrollable sobbing upon hearing of the tragedy. My father's cries were so heart-rending that my mother's friend across the street came running over to find out what was going on. She saw how he tried to muffle his sobs by escaping into the bedroom closet. Though he pushed himself into the clothes, he could not stifle the wailing born of his unbearable pain.

My father sat *shivah* only a few short hours since the mourning period ends when a *yom tov* arrives. He davened in shul as usual for the congregation on Rosh HaShanah. Boruch and his family were staying with our parents over *yom tov* since Boruch was sick with a high fever. When Father came home from shul, he blew shofar for my brother.

Thus ended the life of an inspiring and good-hearted person, Rabbi Yisroel Rabinowicz. He is buried in the

Nachalat Yitzchak Cemetery in Tel Aviv, where the Bahusha Rebbe and other family members of the Ruzhin dynasty are buried.

After my uncle's passing, my father was very concerned for Mime Suranu's welfare. Whenever he came to Eretz Yisrael, he visited her and made sure that she had help at home. In 1984, the year my parents made aliyah, they were appointed by the court of Tel Aviv as her guardians. Father provided whatever she needed until the end of her life.

Reb Yisroel did not have any children of his own, but he had been a very warm and lovable person, and he was my favorite uncle. I named my fifth child, Yisroel, after him.

Almost ten years later, my father's older brother, the Skolyer Rebbe, passed away. When he came to the United States, before the outbreak of World War II, the Fetter Skolyer Rebbe, as we called him, lived in the large chassidic community of Williamsburg in Brooklyn. I remember my father taking us to the Rebbe's house on Bedford Avenue when we were little. There were always a lot of people waiting to see the Rebbe, but of course we wouldn't have to wait long to go in. During the time I attended Rebbetzin Kaplan's Bais Yaakov high school in Williamsburg, I got to know my uncle better. By that time I was big enough and independent enough to visit him on my own. During school breaks, I went to see him and discuss my problems with him. He would always take some of his precious time to talk to me.

I was fortunate to have the Fetter Skolyer Rebbe as the *mesader kiddushin* at my wedding. My husband was a *litvishe* Israeli learning in Lakewood when we got engaged. Rav Shneur Kotler, *zt"l,* the Lakewood *rosh yeshivah,* read the *kesubah.* It was so beautiful to see these two opposites, a chassidic Rebbe and a *litvishe rosh yeshivah,* presiding under one *chuppah.*

One thing I noticed as a teen was that the Rebbe was very weak. He would walk across the room so slowly, sometimes stopping on the way to rest. He told me that he felt terribly weak, and he couldn't understand why. Later on in his life, after I was married, he was diagnosed with cancer of the liver. There was no pain but a lot of weakness. Perhaps it had started years earlier when he felt so drained of strength.

The Rebbe underwent treatments for his cancer, but they were unable to stop its growth. When the doctors felt that his illness was terminal, my father decided to fly him to a doctor in England who used nonconventional methods of healing. Because his brother's condition was so serious, my father, together with several others, booked a flight on a Concorde, which would reach England in two hours instead of the usual eight. No expense or undertaking was too great for my father. He traveled with his brother to England and remained with him through the end.

My uncle had come for treatment in a very advanced state of illness. A few days before his passing, he said that he wanted no *hespedim* said at his *levayah.* On his tombstone he wanted no epitaphs inscribed, just the names of the *sefarim* he had written.

My father spent most of the time at his brother's bedside. That last day he left the room to daven *minchah.* When he returned, my uncle was no longer in this world. Father was broken over the fact that he hadn't been with his brother at the time of his passing. It was the sixth of Shevat 5739 (1979).

The Rebbe's body was taken to Eretz Yisrael. Thousands of Jews attended the *levayah.* He was buried on Har HaZeisim, not far from where my father was buried years later. At the *levayah,* my father announced that the Rebbe's grandson, Reb Avrohom Moshe Rabinowicz, would carry on as the new Skolyer Rebbe.

Our youngest son was named after the Skolyer Rebbe. That was the last bris we made in Bnei Brak. By that time my parents were living in Yerushalayim. (For Mother the *simchah* was not such a happy occasion. Her grandson was born on the day of the *levayah* of her sister Chaya.)

And so, now that Father's two brothers and Mime Perele were no longer alive, and his other sisters were living in homes or close to their children and relatives, the time was ripe for my parents to finally make the move.

On one of their trips to Eretz Yisrael, they found and purchased an apartment in Bayit Vegan, a neighborhood in Yerushalayim. During their visits to Bayit Vegan they made a point of going to see Rav Abramsky, who had been so instrumental in the founding of the Northwest London Jewish Day School back when my parents were living in London.

The new apartment required some renovations to fit my parents' needs. My sister Chavi, who lived in Bayit Vegan, saw to the renovations, while my parents went back home to sell the house and the business and to pack up. They booked a flight for just before the holiday of Shavuos.

I had moved back to Eretz Yisrael with my family in 1980. We were really excited that my parents would be with us shortly. Prior to their move, I flew to the United States to help my mother with the huge task of packing up the home that they had lived in for over thirty years. It was not an easy job, deciding what to keep, what to throw out or give away. I remember finding my mother's wedding gown in the deep closet under the stairs, and as much as I felt a nostalgic connection to it (we had had a good time with that dress on Purim!), it got left behind.

The Rabinowiczes would be missed by their community. The members of the Sefardishe Shul made them a goodbye party, and Rabbi Singer expressed the feelings of all those present in his heartfelt words of farewell.

I remember well the day they left. There was a car waiting to take them to the airport. My father stood in the front doorway of the house, moving his lips silently. He was saying a *tefillah* before leaving the house that had served him as a home for so many years.

"Kim shoin, Mechele! De taxi vart. Come already, Mechele! The taxi is waiting." My mother was impatient. She had been waiting for this moment for years.

But my father continued praying and swaying slightly. He was transfixed by whatever it was he was saying. After all, this house had served him well in so many different capacities over the years. Leaving it forever was not a simple thing. It says in the Gemara that even the homes and houses of learning of the tzaddikim will be resurrected during *techiyas hameisim,* the resurrection of the dead, for they are the vehicles of many acts of righteousness. Although the house is no longer standing today, I might be happily surprised to meet with it once again in the future life!

I never asked my father what it was he was saying during that pivotal moment of his life, and till today I wonder about it.

My parents had sent off a container of their possessions by ship. The container was scheduled to arrive after them. The furniture they had acquired while living in London and had come with them to the United States would now accompany them to their last home. As long as the furniture was still usable, it was good enough for them. This quality of Father's, of constantly being a giver to others but needing very little for himself, was recurrent throughout his life. No matter how shaky those chairs were or how often they needed to be nailed together, Father felt no need to replace them.

Whenever my father came to Israel, he never wanted to be a guest or even to eat in someone's house. It was not his custom to take from others. In a sense, my mother was like that, too. She never wanted anyone to trouble himself for her. Therefore, immediately upon their arrival, my parents checked into the Central Hotel, in the heart of Jerusalem. One of the first things my father did was to go to one of the Judaic shops in Meah She'arim, an old, religious section of Jerusalem, to buy mezuzos for the house. He asked the man in the shop to give him the best mezuzos he had. The man took some out of a drawer.

"These are very high-quality mezuzos," he said. "They were made by a very meticulous *sofer.* He has a good name in the field."

My father examined them and was impressed with the script. "I would like to speak to the *sofer.*"

"I'll give him a call," the shop owner said and dialed the number.

My father arranged to meet the scribe, Reb Velvel Gottlieb, in his home, which was nearby in Meah She'arim. Reb Velvel was surprised that my father didn't ask him to come to the hotel for the meeting. At the designated time, my father arrived at the old stone house, climbed to the fourth floor, and knocked.

Reb Velvel opened the door. "Mr. Rabinowicz?" (My father never wanted people to call him rabbi.)

"Yes. *Shalom aleichem.*"

"Come in. Please sit down." Reb Velvel ushered Father into his small dining room.

"So nice to meet you, Reb Velvel," my father said. "I was very pleased with the *kesav* of the mezuzos that I examined for my new home in Yerushalayim. But I wished to meet the *sofer* himself and talk with him."

He wanted to see whether the man was a *yerei Shamayim*. That is one of the necessary attributes of a scribe, that he write for the sake of Heaven and with extreme care. My father's approach was "*k'minhag hachassidim,*" as the custom of those who are meticulous in their observance of mitzvos and do more than is required by law. Only after speaking with Reb Velvel did he buy the mezuzos.

Reb Velvel was impressed that someone would go out of his way for a stringency almost no one keeps today. They spoke of various things, and my father got to know the man and liked what he saw.

"Reb Velvel, do you think you could come to my apartment and help me put up the mezuzos since I have no hammer with which to do it myself?" he asked him. "I will pay you for your time."

"I will be happy to do it," Reb Velvel answered.

They met at the apartment, which was still nearly bare. My parents were waiting to get some basic furniture before moving in.

"I want to knock the nails into the mezuzah holders myself," my father said to Reb Velvel. "Since the house is mine, the mitzvah is mine to fulfill." Reb Velvel helped him do it.

After that they became good friends. Reb Velvel thought

this was an interesting phenomenon. After all, he was just the scribe of Reb Mechel's mezuzos, and he felt that my father was a very special individual. Theirs was a friendship that was to last until the end of my father's life.

Settling In

The apartment in Bayit Vegan consisted of three bedrooms, a dining room, and the kitchen. One of the rooms was converted into a study for Father. Bookcases were built for his *sefarim* along most of the study walls as well as an *aron kodesh*. Father had acquired one of Reb Yisroel's *sifrei Torah* after his passing, and Mother, years earlier, had been given a very tiny Torah scroll that had belonged to her grandfather, the Yasser Rebbe. In order to accommodate the two Torah scrolls, my father had the *aron kodesh* built in his study.

In the early weeks after they arrived, before the container came from America, the apartment was furnished with some furniture from the Jewish Agency and odds and ends borrowed from neighbors. Despite the primitive conditions, my parents were happy to be in Eretz Yisrael. From the dining-room balcony at the back of the house, a great panorama spread out below them as the land sloped downward. They would sit on the small balcony, watching the lights twinkle in the dusk as night settled over Yerushalayim. They breathed deeply of the air of the Holy Land, just enjoying being there.

"*A mechayah tzie zitzen du* — Such a pleasure to sit here," Father exclaimed. "*A nes mir hobben du gekimen* — It's a miracle that we moved here!" Mother could only agree with him.

It was a most interesting phenomenon. At home in New York, my father was a well-known personality. Countless times he acted as the guest of honor at fund-raising functions and was awarded plaques and other symbols of appreciation. His desk drawers were full of the speeches he had written for these occasions. As much as he ran away from honor, it pursued him. Here in Yerushalayim, who knew him, who would relate to him, let alone accord him honor? It would seem that here he would feel as if in *galus*, in exile, rather than in New York. But it was just the opposite. He said that it was good to be in Eretz Yisrael. My mother was forever grateful that he had the merit to live there for ten years.

Right from the beginning people recognized that there was something special about my father. Even before my parents actually moved to Bayit Vegan, on one of their visits, when Father went to the Chassidim Shul, the *gabbai* gave him a place by the eastern wall, the area reserved for prominent or learned people. Somehow my father transmitted the sense that he was a special person.

Once my mother and father were going somewhere by taxi. My father got out and my mother after him. A passerby followed Father with his eyes. When he saw that Mother was with him, he stopped her and asked, "Who is this man?"

My mother replied simply, "A Jew who has come to live in Eretz Yisrael."

"But who is he? What is he?"

My mother couldn't convince him that he was "just a Jew." He was sure that my father was someone special.

The people who met my father after he moved to Bayit Vegan did not know him as the vital, enthusiastic doer that he was. They knew him as a retired man who mostly stayed at home. Even so, they got to know something of his personality as he made himself felt in the community. It came out in shul, in his *mesiras nefesh*, his unflinching dedication, to get to shul every day despite his growing frailty, in his *mesiras nefesh* to go to the mikveh, in his davening on Rosh HaShanah for the congregation, in his *tzedakah*, in his love of Torah learning, in the *seudos* he made at home for others, in his general love of mitzvos, and in his cheerful demeanor. There was a lot that those who got to know him could learn from him, even in his retirement and severely compromised physical state.

Immediately upon my father's arrival, two people came to visit him. The first day my parents moved in, Rav Chaim Porush, author of the *sefer Peirush Chai*, came to the door and said that he had heard that new *olim* had arrived. He asked if he could be of help in any way. After moving to Eretz Yisrael, Father continued his custom of having *simchas yom tov* and *seudos* in his home, and Rav Porush always attended. Occasionally Father would make a *seudah* in a hall, such as on the *yahrtzeit* of his father, where he would also make a *siyum mishnayos*. When Father stopped having them and no longer sent out invitations, Rav Porush, remembering the dates, would ask if there was going to be a *seudah* or not.

Rav Schleisinger of Yeshivas Kol Torah came that first day as well. Eventually my father got to know all of the local *rabbanim*. Besides Rav Schleisinger, there was Rav Kundstaat of Yeshivas Kol Torah, Rav Zilberberg of the Chassidim Shul, and Rav Ginsburg of the Ninety-nine Shul. They were happy to make his acquaintance and helped my parents in any way they could.

Rav Kundstaat spent time visiting and talking to my father. He not only had the financial welfare of the yeshivah in mind during his visits, but he sincerely wanted to help my parents. On more than one occasion he went out of his way to be of assistance to them. My nephew Yisrael Silverman learned in the *yeshivah ketanah* of Kol Torah. For the boy's bar mitzvah, Rav Kundstaat arranged that my parents spend Shabbos in one of the rooms in the yeshivah so that they would not have to walk over on Shabbos. They declined his kind offer, but appreciated that Rav Kundstaat had thought of them.

Rav Schleisinger was not involved with the financial affairs of the yeshivah. When visiting my father, he had no interests in mind other than that of fulfilling a mitzvah, coming for the pure sake of doing a *chesed*. He came even when it was hard for my father to hear and a visitor had to work hard at being understood. My mother became friendly with Rebbetzin Schleisinger and Rebbetzin Ginsburg, enjoying the company of these two wonderful women.

Rav Schleisinger made it a habit to visit my father regularly. My parents always asked him for advice, such as which butcher to buy meat from and which *rav* they should use for selling their *chametz* before Pesach. It was a relationship of mutual respect. Rav Schleisinger told me that he could tell that my father was a *"ben adam chashuv mechubad v'talmid chacham,"* an important personality, honorable, and a Torah scholar. He said once, "I heard it said that HaRav Shlomo Zalman Auerbach, *zatzal*, remarked that your father was a distinguished person and a *talmid chacham*." Even after my father's passing, Rav Schleisinger would come to the house to ask my mother how she was doing, and for years the Schleisingers continued sending my mother *mishlo'ach manos* on Purim.

Once my parents settled in, my father made a *chanukas habayis*, a housebreaking celebration. Although he had arrived in Eretz Yisrael not long before, people got to know him almost immediately. Avrumi Nadav attended the *chanukas habayis* and said he could not believe how many people were there even though Father was a newcomer to the community.

At first Father davened at the Chassidim Shul on HaPisgah Street. On Simchas Torah he was given the honor of *chasan Bereishis,* as he had in New York. And, as he had done in New York, he would make a Kiddush in his house and give a Torah discourse in his unique way. When it became more and more difficult for him to walk, and going that distance was too much for him, he started davening in a shul down the street at 99 Bayit Vegan Street. The shul was commonly called the "Ninety-nine Shul." There, too, he received the honor of *chasan Bereishis.* And it was there that my father davened *shacharis* for the congregation on Rosh HaShanah.

Once, on Rosh HaShanah night, when it had already become very hard for my father to walk, he was late for davening. He went to some other shul, and my mother and Yisrael had no idea where he was. Much later that night someone brought him home. He had walked to the Sochotchov shul to daven. It was located on Chidah Street, and a healthy adult could easily do the walk in ten or fifteen minutes. But my father walked very slowly, and it took him over an hour. After davening, he became confused and could not find his way back. Quite a bit later, someone brought him home.

In the later years of his life, Father was nearly blind, hard of hearing, could barely walk, and had episodes of confusion — yet nothing would stop him from fulfilling Hashem's mitzvos.

The Kollel

One day, several weeks after they had met, my father called up Reb Velvel. He had something to talk about and wanted to meet him at the hotel.

"Reb Velvel," my father said when the *sofer* arrived, "I have always finished a certain amount of learning every day. Nowadays it is very hard for me to learn because I cannot see well. Reading has become very difficult, almost impossible. I do not want to forgo the reward one earns by learning Torah. Therefore, I wish to set up an evening *kollel* in which the young men will learn in my merit."

My father had a deep love of learning and throughout his life had pushed himself relentlessly to complete his daily *seder*. He always wore very thick glasses, and for the last few years he was considered legally blind. Now, in his old age, his eyes were letting him down. Reading had become almost impossible. I remember how my father would try to learn, removing his glasses and holding the *sefer* extremely close to his face. He knew he could no longer learn very much other than what he knew by heart.

My father explained what he wanted to Reb Velvel.

"I will pay ten young men and a *rosh kollel* to learn for one and a half hours each evening. I am willing to pay them eighty dollars a month and the *rosh kollel* one hundred and fifty dollars a month. During the months of Tishrei and Nissan, in honor of *yom tov*, I will pay twice that amount. This will be done with the understanding that the merit of their learning will go into my account in Heaven. The *rosh kollel* will be responsible for seeing that the ten men do their allotted learning in the time and place he sets up for them. Do you know someone who could undertake this project for me?"

"I would be happy to find the ten men for you and to be their *mashgiach,* to make sure they come on time and learn as they should," Reb Velvel answered. "I even know a shul we could use for this purpose." My father and Reb Velvel shook hands on it.

To the impoverished Yerushalmi men, learning Torah in financially difficult straits, an offer such as this must have seemed heaven-sent. For my father, having eleven serious Torah scholars learning in his merit must also have seemed heaven-sent. He was by no means a wealthy man when he moved to Eretz Yisrael, yet he used his money for what he thought was important. Establishing the *kollel* and giving funds to charity was one of the priorities of his life.

Once Reb Velvel got the ten men together Father had each of them sign a contract. It stipulated that this was a business transaction, as made by Yissachar and Zevulun, in which my father gave them their monthly stipend in return for their learning in his merit. He told them that if they cheated on their learning time it was as though they were stealing from him. He was literally buying hours of learning from them since he could no longer learn as he had in the past.

My father appeared at the *kollel* each Rosh Chodesh to give the men their monthly stipend. No matter what was going on, rain or shine, he'd be there. He was very particular to pay the men on time, and Reb Velvel claimed that it couldn't have been more than a handful of times over the years that he paid late. He used this visit to spend time with the men in Torah discussion. The spiritual satisfaction he felt from these interactions was obvious to all. These men were like his children, and he kept in touch with each one of them.

" '*Chochmaso ansah bo* — His wisdom testified for him,' " Reb Velvel told me. "You could see on his face that he was a *talmid chacham*, a Torah scholar. The wisdom lit up his face. But it wasn't only that. We all knew it from the things he said, from the Torah he spoke when he joined us in our learning. Whenever I talked to him, in whichever subject it was, you saw it. He was fluent in all of *Shas*.

"Your father once told me," he said, "that he had learned through the entire *Shas* five times.

" '*Ribbono shel olam*! When did you have time to do that?' I asked him, amazed. 'You were always busy with your business.'

"'That's right,' he said to me. 'I spent a lot of time flying on planes. I used that time to learn. Sitting in airports between flights, I learned. Waiting for customers to arrive for their appointments, I learned. When you look for the time you need, you find it!'

"He made it sound so easy," Reb Velvel concluded. "He had a sharp mind, and he comprehended the Gemara quickly. Thus he was able to do something that is no simple matter for even a full-time learner."

The *kollel* grew over time until it included fifteen men. Reb Velvel said the men learned well together and enjoyed learning as a group. The *kollel* continued for six years. At that point my mother realized that they could no longer afford it. Once the *kollel* was disbanded, the young men actually missed it — not the extra money, but the feeling of closeness and *geshmak*, the sweetness of the learning, that they had experienced together.

Reb Velvel alone continued to receive a monthly fee to learn in Father's merit, and he remained a friend of the family.

Sefer Zimras HaAretz

My father had always written down his *chiddushei Torah,* his original Torah insights, but none of them were organized. When he finally published his *sefer* based on the *shiurim* he had given over the years, he told Avrumi Nadav that this was the little bit of his Torah insights that he had left in writing.

Once a large manila envelope full of his handwritten *chiddushim,* which he had taken with him to the country in upstate New York, got lost. Apparently the envelope fell out of the taxi, because when my parents were unpacking, he could not find it. He immediately put an ad in the paper promising a large reward to anyone who brought him his precious envelope. No one came forward. The loss was permanent and caused him great distress.

Rabbi Yisrael Spiegel, an editor for the *Hamodia* newspaper, was a neighbor of my parents in Bayit Vegan. My father got to know him shortly after my parents moved in. Rabbi Spiegel himself was a born-and-bred Yerushalmi Jew and a Chortkover chassid. Chortkov is a branch of the Ruzhiner dynasty, and so Rabbi Spiegel was inclined to visit my parents and talk about the family history on his and Mother's sides. Rabbi Spiegel felt he had a common background with Reb Mechel, since his father was from Galicia, like my father's family. Father's davening on Rosh HaShanah reminded him of the *niggunim* of the *"alte heim,"* the old country.

My father decided, with my mother's prompting, to give

Rabbi Spiegel the job of turning the many brief notes of his *shiurim* into a *sefer*. These were based on many of the *divrei Torah* he had said over the years at Congregation Anshei Sefard and at home on Shabbos. My father's notes were basically outlines of his *shiurim*, with very short points that he expanded upon as he spoke. The editor was required to look up the source material of the subject mentioned and write out in length what my father was referring to in his outline. He would also need to compile a listing of all the source material for the reader.

As he took on the project, Rabbi Spiegel said he could see that my father knew a lot. He had widespread knowledge of the Rambam's writings, Talmud, and the works of Chassidus. He included in his Torah insights wisdom, *drush*, and Kabbalah. He had insights that were like riddles, like a "*blitz in mo'ach*," as Rabbi Spiegel put it, sparks of lightning in one's mind.

Putting the *sefer* together was a tremendous undertaking. Rabbi Spiegel had his sons and son-in-law, young men learning in *kollel*, join him in the project. The young men expressed their wonder at the beautiful Torah thoughts my father had produced, saying, "What kind of a person is this?" Writing the *sefer* took several years; it was published in 1989.

Father chose the name *Zimras HaAretz* for his sefer because the *gematriah* of the word *zimras* equals that of his name, Yechiel Mechel ben Boruch Pinchas. In the foreword, he wrote that he was given the ability to produce this work in the merit of his forefathers, and especially in the merit of his father, Reb Boruch Pinchas, the Skolyer Rebbe. On the page preceding the foreword, he expressed his thanks to my mother for being at his side over the years and supporting him in his Torah learning. He asked that Hashem help him see *nachas* from their children.

There was a most interesting note on the flyleaf of the book. In it the author informed the public that the *sefer* was being distributed for free and that he did not wish to receive payment for it. His intention was only to publicize words of Torah without accruing any personal gain for himself.

He had five hundred copies printed up completely at his expense. Whenever a yeshivah boy or even a cheder boy came to the door to ask for the *sefer*, my mother or father would give one away. So many little boys came that after a while my mother said to them, "Only from bar mitzvah age and up."

Rabbi Spiegel felt my father was a unique person. He was a businessman, and yet he built a world of Torah and Chassidus. He said that in truth he had the personality and essence of a Rebbe, and that is why he was so honored by all who knew him.

A Special Zeidy

The immediate benefactors of my parents' move to Eretz Yisrael were my sister Chava Silverman and her two children, Rachel and Yisrael. Chavi was divorced, and the family always came to eat at my parents' on Shabbos. My father served as something of a father figure for the children, although he was in his seventies when he moved there. Rachel was ten years old when she got to know her grandfather and thought that "Zeidy was a tzaddik." Yisrael was eight years old and would go with his *zeidy* to shul.

Once Yisrael wanted to buy a set of *Shulchan Aruch*,

which cost 250 shekels. He had been saving his money for a long time but was still fifty shekels short. He figured he would borrow the money from his *zeidy* and pay him back when he earned it.

"Hello, Zeidy. How are you?" Yisrael said to my father when he came to visit.

"*Baruch Hashem, zeier fein.* Very well. How are you?"

"Good, *baruch Hashem.* Zeidy, I'm saving money to buy a set of *Shulchan Aruch,* and I am still short fifty shekels..."

Before he could say another word, his *zeidy* took out the money from his pocket. Handing him the bill, he said, "I'll give it to you. Here. Go buy it and learn good!" Yisrael understood that it would have been insulting to his grandfather had he suggested paying him back.

Once my father went out to buy an *esrog* and *lulav* for himself in Bayit Vegan. He came back after a long time with his precious purchases. After putting them safely away, he sat down to rest. Suddenly he got up and prepared to leave the house again.

"Mechele," my mother said, perplexed, "where are you going?"

"I promised to buy an *esrog* and *lulav* for Yisrael, and I forgot. I must go back now and take care of it."

"But you're so tired, Mechele. You just spent so much time walking around trying to find your own *esrog* and *lulav.* Why don't you go tomorrow?"

"Yisrael will come over and see that I have my *esrog* and *lulav* already, and he'll be sure that his are here, too. He will be really disappointed if he sees that I bought mine and I didn't buy his."

My father wouldn't let his tiredness get in the way of his concern over a little boy's disappointment.

When walking became harder for my father and Yisrael was older, he gave the job of choosing an *esrog* and *lulav* to his grandson. One year Yisrael went to one of the local merchants, an American by the name of Mr. Beer, who knew my father from Boro Park.

"Hello, Mr. Beer. I am Mr. Rabinowicz's grandson. I came to buy an *esrog* and *lulav* for him."

"Mr. Rabinowicz!" the man exclaimed. "What do you mean, 'Mr. Rabinowicz'? Do you know who your grandfather is? Do you know what Rabbi Rabinowicz did for us in Boro Park and all over greater New York? How can you call him 'Mr. Rabinowicz'?"

Yisrael, embarrassed, corrected himself hurriedly. What Mr. Beer did not know was that my father wanted people to call him "Mr. Rabinowicz." He shied away from titles such as rabbi. He was never interested in personal honor.

During the last few years of his life, my father and mother went to the Tamir Hotel for Pesach and invited Chavi and the children to join them. On one such occasion they were sitting in the dining room, and my father noticed the many other *chassidishe* guests. He turned to Yisrael, saying that it was high time he put on a *bekeshe*. Yisrael, still a child and not particularly skilled in the art of tact, answered that he was not a chassid.

"Don't say that!" his grandfather replied emphatically. "Do you know who your great-grandfather and great-great-grandfather were? Do you know who Reb Boruch of Yampela was?" He proceeded to name all of the generations right up to the Ba'al Shem Tov. He told Yisrael that if he would learn the *sefarim* of these holy people he would become a big *talmid chacham*.

I'm sure the conversation was very enlightening, but Yisrael remained a *litvak*. He said that this was the only time he remembered his *zeidy* criticizing him for something. He never remembered his *zeidy* getting angry at any one of them, at Bubby, Chavi, him, or Rachel. Zeidy might sometimes get angry when defending the honor of Heaven, but never at the family.

Hachnasas Sefer Torah

In the beginning of their friendship, my father revealed to Reb Velvel another one of his aspirations: he wanted to have a *sefer Torah* written. He asked Reb Velvel to do it. Reb Velvel was a busy scribe, and he was unable to get started on the Torah scroll right away. It was a few years before he began, and it took him a year and a half to complete. On the day Reb Velvel completed the Torah scroll, it was brought to Father's home in Bayit Vegan.

Father had invited many people by written invitation to attend the ceremony. We lived in Bnei Brak then and came to be at the ceremony, as did Boruch from the United States.

The last few words of the *sefer Torah* still had to be written. Various people were given the honor of writing a letter of the Torah under the watchful guidance of the scribe.

My father wrote out the last four words of the Torah, "*Moshe l'einei kol Yisrael.*" He had pointed out to us, many years earlier, that the first letter of each of these last four words, *mem, yud, chaf, lamed,* spelled his name, Mechel. Writing the words that formed his name while fulfilling the mitzvah of having a kosher Torah scroll written must have been a most inspiring experience for him.

Mother in Bayit Vegan

Father lighting Chanukah candles in Bayit Vegan

My parents being honored at a dinner for Ohel, December 1981

Father being honored by Kollel Chibas Yerushalayim

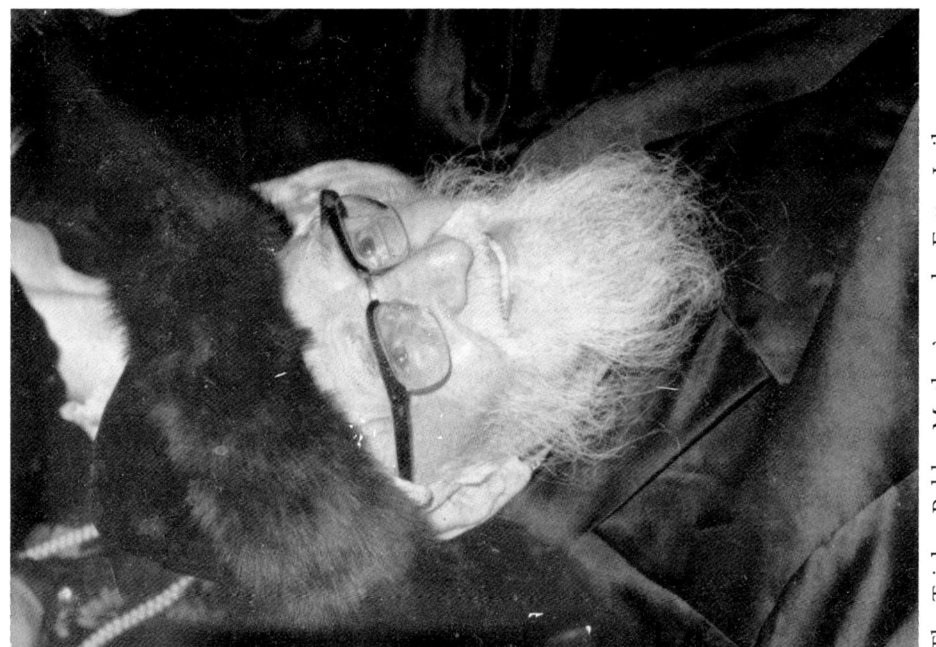

The Trisker Rebbe, Mother's uncle, Fetter Leibenu

One of Father's many *tzedakah* projects in Eretz Yisrael

Father in Bayit Vegan

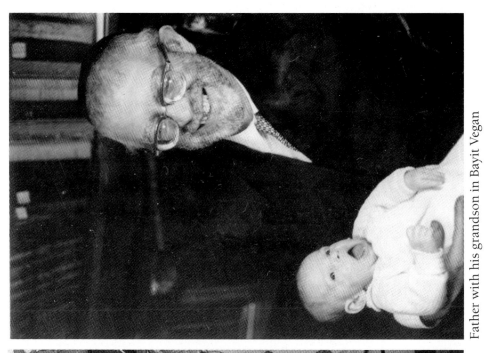

Father with his grandson in Bayit Vegan

Enjoying the Toporowitch grandchildren in Bayit Vegan

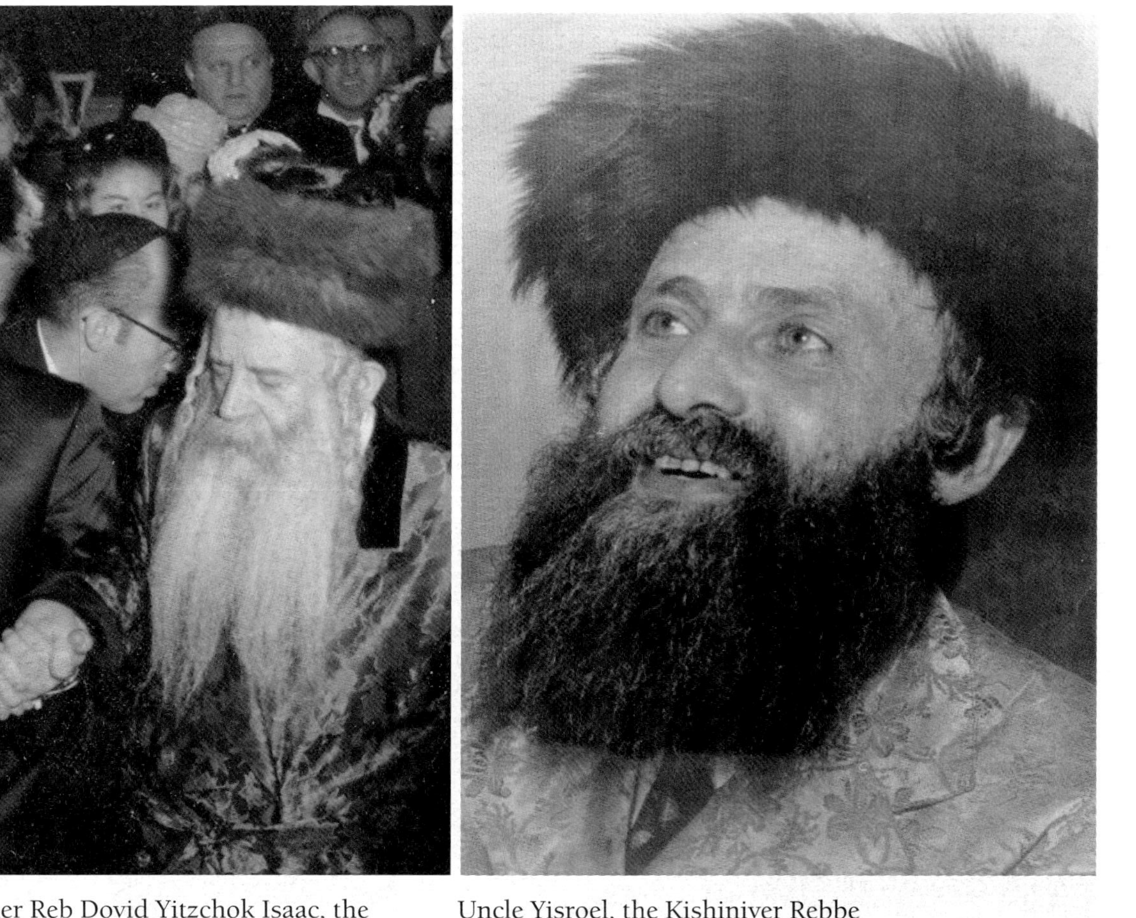

Father with his brother Reb Dovid Yitzchok Isaac, the Skolyer Rebbe

Uncle Yisroel, the Kishiniver Rebbe

Father blessing his granddaughter Shainy at her wedding in Bnei Brak

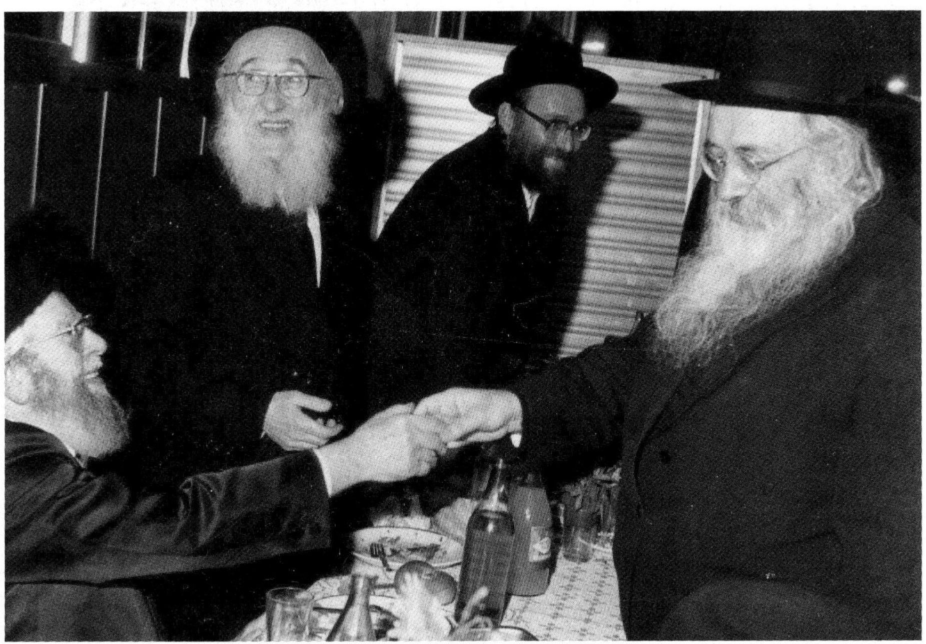

At Shainy's wedding, from right to left: Father, Rabbi Refael Yitzchak Wasserman, Rabbi Shmuel Nadel (Shainy's father-in-law), and Rabbi Chaim Greineman

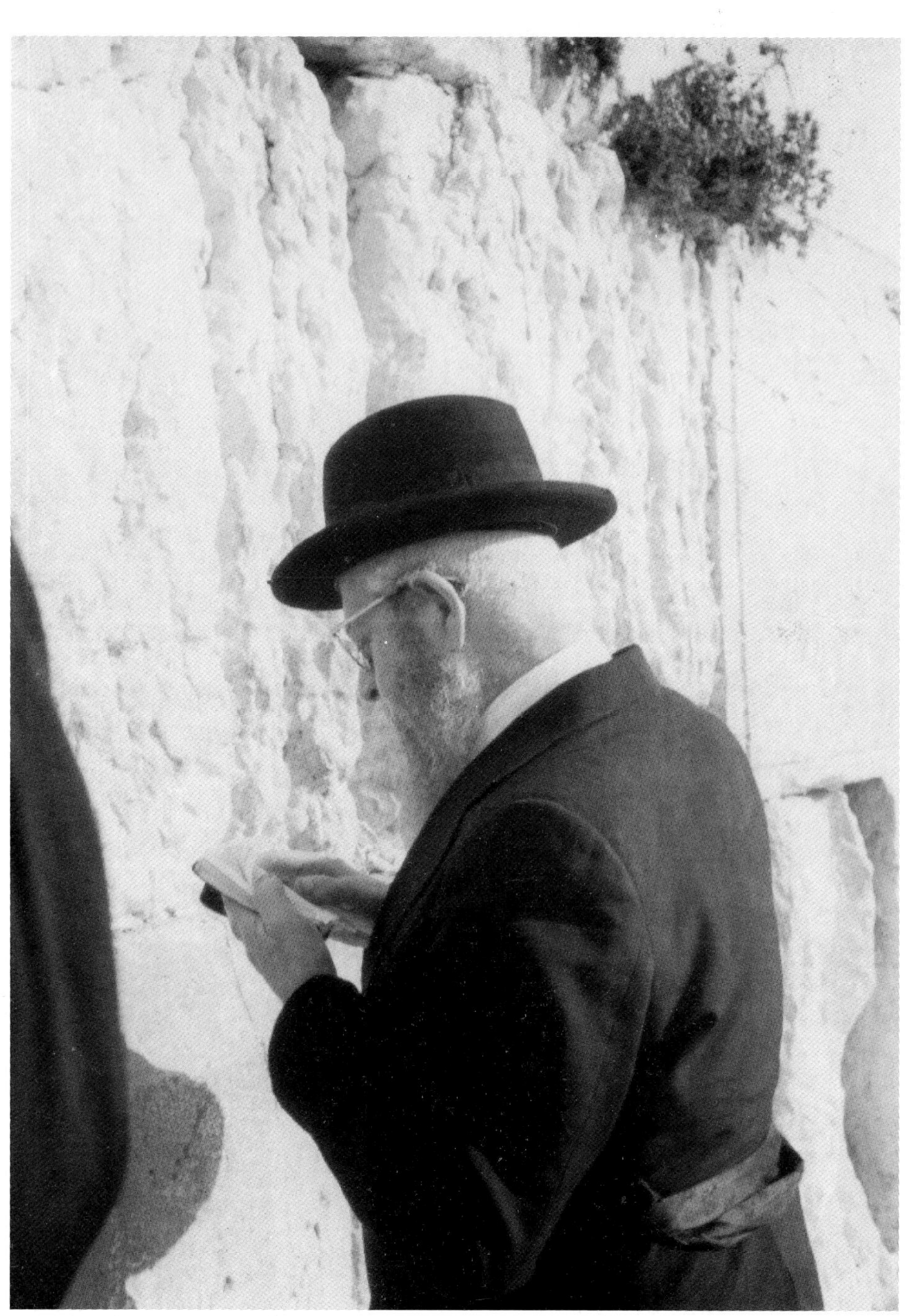
At the Kosel

After it was completed, the *sefer Torah* was wrapped in a tallis, and Boruch carried it under a *chuppah,* a wedding canopy, to the Ninety-nine Shul down the street. Cheder boys were given burning torches to hold, and a long procession went singing and dancing toward the shul. Police closed off the street so that the traffic would not interfere with the procession. Although my father was old at the time and it was hard for him to walk, he led the procession with energy and joy alongside the Torah scroll. We all commented to each other, "Look how well Deddy is walking!"

The joyous occasion invigorated him. His face was glowing. Not many people have the merit of having a *sefer Torah* written. My father loved the mitzvos so deeply, and doing one as impressive as this must have been a tremendous inspiration for him. It was truly a momentous occasion for our family, creating a strong impression in our minds.

At the *seudah* following the *hachnasas sefer Torah* in the Ninety-nine Shul, Rabbi Ginsburg spoke. He said that people had a "smell" for where the money was; they always knew where to go when they needed *tzedakah.* And they knew that my father was an address for *tzedakah.* But at the same time, he was a *talmid chacham,* a Torah scholar. He had "*Torah v'gedulah b'makom echad* — Torah learning and riches in one place."

The Torah scroll was given to the Ninety-nine Shul for as long as Father was alive. The *gabbai* of the shul wrote a beautiful letter expressing his thanks for the use of the *sefer Torah.* After my father's passing, during the *shivah,* the *sefer Torah* was brought to the house and used for *krias haTorah.* Later Mother gave it to a relative, Rabbi Friedman, the Bahusha Rebbe in Bnei Brak, who had both a shul and a *kollel.* My mother was only too happy to give the Bahusha Rebbe my father's beloved *sefer Torah*; this young relative had established a place of learning and *kedushah*. He was the grandson of the Bahusha Rebbe of Romania (and later of Tel Aviv), whose home had been a refuge for countless Jews fleeing the Nazis.

The Beloved Mitzvah of Mikveh

When Father was younger, there was no such a thing as davening *shacharis* without going to the mikveh first. In Eretz Yisrael he made it a point of going to the mikveh on *erev Shabbos*. But walking there was becoming harder and harder for him. One day my father met the Tolner Rebbe, a distant relative of Mother's who lived in Bayit Vegan. He was an old man at that time, and he had built a mikveh in his house. He told my father how good it was. It was so convenient. *What a wonderful idea,* Father thought to himself.

"I have decided to build a mikveh in the house," he announced one day to my mother.

"Where?" she asked incredulously.

"I'll build a partition in the study, and it will be there in the corner."

"The room is so small as it is. How is it going to fit?"

"I took the measurements already. There's more than enough room," he said with finality.

That was that. When my father decided to do something, it was as good as done.

He knew what building a mikveh entailed since he had his experiences from the London and Boro Park mikvehs. He contacted an engineer and a contractor. The building was an old one, and the engineer had to verify if the floor — the ceiling of the apartment below — could carry the added weight of the water of the mikveh. Constructing it was a major feat of engineering since the space was so limited. He had to figure out exactly how to build it, with steps leading up and then steps leading down into the mikveh. The contractor had to be sure that the waterproofing was solid so that there would be no leakages to the neighbors below. Plumbing for hot and cold water had to be installed, as well as a drainage system. Handrails were attached to the walls for my father to hold on to, since he was no longer steady on his feet.

All of this he did against my mother's better judgment. The doctor had said that it was dangerous for him to submerge himself under water because of his frequent dizzy spells. But he paid no attention to what the doctor said. He wanted this mikveh so much that he spared no expense. According to Reb Velvel, it cost him about ten thousand dollars to have it made!

Besides using the mikveh on *erev Shabbos*, he also used it on *erev Yom Kippur* after the *seudah hamafsekes*, the last meal before the fast begins. He had a custom, brought down in *sefarim*, to immerse in the mikveh after the meal and to say the *vidui* prayer, as one does during *minchah* on *erev Yom Kippur.*

But my mother was worried about Father's infirmity in his legs, and it came to the point that Mother had the plumber disconnect the plumbing of the mikveh. Since Father was not using his own mikveh anymore, he started using the public mikveh again. That was my father — a fighter to the end for what he decided he had to do.

Sometimes on *erev Shabbos* he wanted to go to the

mikveh when it was already quite late. My mother would ask him not to go, but he felt that he had to. It could take him half an hour to walk from the taxi the short distance into the mikveh, even though people helped him. He'd come home just before candle lighting. But he just couldn't give up going to the mikveh; it meant that much to him.

Once it was a few minutes before candle lighting, and my father hadn't come home yet. My mother was terribly upset. She called Yisrael.

"Yisrael, sweetheart, Zeidy is not home. I don't know where he is. Could you please go and look for him?"

Yisrael ran over to the mikveh, and sure enough his grandfather was there. A few people were helping him walk out. When Yisrael appeared on the scene, they yelled at him how irresponsible he was to let an old man go to the mikveh alone. Someone took them home by car. After that incident Mother was on the lookout every *erev Shabbos*, making sure that Father would not disappear on her. It hurt him deeply; he did not understand that it was no longer safe for him to go to the mikveh.

The Gulf War

The Gulf War broke out in January 1991. The official date for the outbreak of the war was meant to be January 15, the day the Americans planned to attack Iraq in the event that Iraq refused to retreat from Kuwait. However, the Arabs preempted the Americans by sending their first rocket against Israel the Shabbos before the deadline.

People were in a state of terror, not knowing what the future would bring. Many could not sleep, since often the dreaded Scuds were sent at night. Attacking on Shabbos was another way the *resha'im* created havoc, disturbing the peace and harmony of the Jewish day of rest.

Tel Aviv was the target of most of the bombings, since it was the financial and social hub of the nation. All of my married children lived in Bnei Brak at that time, which was quite close to Tel Aviv, and sometimes they could actually see the Scuds flying toward Tel Aviv and the Patriot missiles intercepting them. Often the shocks of the impact of the Scuds and Patriots or the falling pieces of missiles from the in-air interceptions sent tremors through Bnei Brak homes.

It happened once that a piece of a shattered Scud fell into the yard of a synagogue in Bnei Brak. Interestingly, the name of the synagogue is Kisei Rachamim, "Seat of Mercy," and, as divine intervention would have it, no one was hurt. On another occasion, a missile made a direct hit on a house in Ramat Yitzchak, a small borough of Tel Aviv bordering Bnei Brak, causing windows and doors of Bnei Brak houses to fall out. The occupants had to evacuate until their homes could be repaired. People walked around in fear. Many American families living in Israel and American students left for home.

After a while it became apparent that Iraq was not bombing Yerushalayim. Yerushalayim had a large Arab population, and, most importantly, the holiest Arab sites were situated there. Tel Aviv residents began streaming to Yerushalayim to spend the nights there. It has been said that each night something like ten thousand outsiders slept in Yerushalayim during the Gulf War and then would travel to work in the morning.

One of my sons-in-law was greatly affected by the pressures of living in a state of war and decided to stay with my parents in Yerushalayim. He and my daughter and baby son moved into my parents' home in Bayit Vegan. The sealed room had been prepared according to government regulations. The special baby crib was set up in the room, and they all had their gas masks. When the siren blared its warning the Shabbos my children were there, everyone but my father rushed into the sealed room.

"*Vos macht men zich narish*? Why are you acting so foolish?" he asked them. My mother's entreaties to him to join them in the sealed room was to no avail. He continued singing *zemiros* as usual. After an hour, the all-clear sounded, and the occupants of the sealed room returned to the Shabbos table.

"*Nu? Vos is geshein?* Well? What happened?" He was absolutely sure in the midst of the fear and confusion that nothing would happen. And nothing did.

My children spent a week with their grandparents, and it must have been inspiring to see my father's steadfast *bitachon* in such a troubled time.

My father never once put on his gas mask during the war. After a while, his calm rubbed off on my mother, and she stopped putting on her gas mask and even going into the sealed room.

The Infirmities of Old Age

Getting used to a new country, to a new mentality, is no easy task for anyone. It was even harder for my parents, who were elderly. My father and mother found the socialized medicine system difficult to deal with, and they started using a private doctor who would come to their house.

My father had all sorts of health problems. During the ten years he lived in Eretz Yisrael, he had his gall bladder removed, underwent spinal surgery, and experienced severe bladder complications. He also suffered from encephalitis, water on the brain. This condition was not painful, but it caused dizziness, confusion, and memory loss. His hearing was rapidly deteriorating, and his sight was close to nil. At some point he bought a hearing aid. Perhaps the volume was too high or perhaps it was too low; perhaps he heard annoying static. He claimed that the hearing aid made funny noises. Whatever the case, he hated it and refused to wear it.

Going out was becoming more and more difficult. Father supported himself with a cane and walked very slowly. Sometimes he used a walker outside. All the taxi drivers knew my father because he had such difficulty walking, and he frequently went, even short distances, by taxi. Whenever I took a taxi to the hospital before my father's *petirah*, I asked the drivers if they knew Mr. Rabinowicz, and invariably they did. They all had good things to say about him. He always treated them respectfully, and they enjoyed his Tanach-like Hebrew.

Walking became so problematic that going the short distance to shul on Shabbos took my father so long that he'd miss a good part of *shacharis*. My mother decided that the best way to ensure that he get to shul on time was to have him taken there by wheelchair, so she paid a high-school girl or boy to push the wheelchair back and forth from shul.

At first it was very hard for Father to allow someone to do this for him, because it pointed out his limitations so vividly. He felt extremely self-conscious and fought the idea for a long time. He didn't feel old, and he wanted to walk, although really he couldn't.

Sometimes he would start walking to shul. Then he would tire and decide to use the wheelchair the rest of the way. Finally he made peace with the situation and got used to the wheelchair. Once he felt comfortable with his new mode of travel, he would wave to the children on the street and greet them.

Sometimes on the way to shul he would say *birkos hashachar* if he hadn't had time to say it at home. As he approached the shul, the men would see him coming. He would get out of the chair and start walking in, and two men would come over to help him the rest of the way in.

My father suffered greatly from his difficulty with walking. The orthopedist said he had a narrowing of the spinal column and recommended surgery of the lumbar spine. It was very risky, but the doctor promised my father that his success rate with this surgery was at least 90 percent. My father desperately wanted to get better, so he went ahead with the surgery. My father was confident that he would recover quickly and regain his former strength. Unfortunately, instead of recovering, he developed thrombosis in one of his legs, and he remained in the hospital for several weeks.

Sadly, after all of his suffering, the surgery did not improve his walking at all. He thought that the Israeli doctor had performed the surgery unsuccessfully. Actually, the problem was that he had narrowing of the spinal column in the vertebra of the neck as well as in the lumbar area, and so the surgery could not have helped him in any event. He would not undergo an operation in the vertebrae of the neck since it entailed a tremendous amount of risk.

In November 1990, Boruch's son, Yossi, got engaged. Boruch wanted our parents to come to the wedding. This was no simple matter due to father's ill health. But Yossi was Boruch's only son, and it meant a lot to Boruch that our parents be there. Both my father and mother came to the wedding. The joy my father experienced from participating in this family *simchah* had a profound influence on him. He was energetic, and he danced at the wedding. He even walked up the three flights of stairs to Boruch's apartment for meals. On Shabbos a non-Jew pushed his wheelchair to the Skolyer shul, where he davened *shacharis* for the congregation. He looked and felt good and enjoyed himself very much.

In Adar of 1990, my father underwent gall bladder surgery. That was the year I moved back to the United States. Later that year, before Pesach, he developed bladder trouble. It was so bad that he was hospitalized, but he was allowed home for Pesach. My father's seder usually stretched well into the night, but that year he did not feel well and finished the seder by ten-thirty. He developed an infection and was running a fever, and on Chol HaMo'ed he returned to the hospital. He spent another few days in the hospital and finally came home. All I could do from the United States was to make frequent telephone calls and daven.

My father was very generous in his old age, as he was when he was younger. The problem was that as he aged he sometimes became detached from reality. He was exhibiting the early stages of Alzheimer's disease. The doctor explained that the encephalitis was causing swelling of his brain, which resulted in his disorientation. He would forget things and misunderstand what was going on. Sometimes he would be completely clear, and at other times he would not remember what he had just done. After I moved back to the United

States, each time I called him up he asked me where I was.

My father began writing checks for large amounts of money that had no coverage or that were clearly not realistic. Reb Boruch Leifer said that in one's old age you can see what the person was like when he was young. My father was always a giver, and now he continued to give beyond his means.

Just as in previous years, people still came to him for *tzedakah*. It was well known that he was a person who gave generously, and his house was always full of people in need of one thing or another. He wrote checks for everyone who came. Unfortunately, there were those who took advantage of him. They would say, "Add another zero, another zero." And he would. His nature was to be a giver, and in his confused state he did not comprehend what his giving entailed.

Another thing my father had to give up was his beloved mitzvah of mikveh. My mother was very worried about his using the mikveh every day at home. The steps going up were steep and narrow, as were the steps leading down into the mikveh. If he would get dizzy and fall, she would not be able to pull him out. The doctor said that under no circumstances should he use the mikveh. So my mother emptied it out and told my father that the doctor had forbidden him to use it. This infuriated him, and he simply filled the mikveh again and used it as usual.

Sometimes he forgot that he had opened the faucets, and the water would overflow and flood the house. After this happened on several occasions, Chavi found an electrician who installed a device that would automatically turn off the flow once the water reached a certain level. My father was very happy to have another electronic gadget on his mikveh.

As Father's condition deteriorated, Mother realized that the situation was very dangerous and had no choice but to call a plumber and have him disconnect the water supply to the mikveh. On several occasions, my father called the plumber to come and "fix" the mikveh. My mother secretly called to cancel the plumber and explain what was going on. For a while, Father raged over this, but before long he got used to the new situation. When his brother-in-law Yossik Schorr approached him to learn Kabbalah with him, he responded sadly that he couldn't do so, since he was no longer immersing in a mikveh on a daily basis.

Alexander

Now that my father was so limited in getting around, my mother hired a Russian man to come several times a week to take him out in the wheelchair. Alexander was a simple Jew who had not had the opportunity to learn about *Yiddishkeit* in Russia. But he spoke Yiddish, and he was a good person who tried to make his boss happy on their walks. My father liked him, and they got on well.

As Alexander pushed him along, people on the street would call to my father. He could not see well and would ask Alexander who the person was.

Alexander usually had no idea who it was, but he didn't want my father to feel that what he said or asked was not important and didn't deserve his serious attention. And so Alexander would make up a name.

"*Ehr heist Moshe*. His name is Moshe."

"*Vus teet ehr?* What does he do?" my father asked.

"*Ehr is a shister*. He's a cobbler."

Alexander would go into a long, detailed account of exactly what that man did, making the whole thing up. Someone else would have gotten annoyed and snapped that he had no idea who these strangers were. But good-natured Alexander found a way to keep my father interested and occupied, and he did it in a very lively and enthusiastic manner.

My parents tried to educate Alexander about Judaism, explaining about the *yamim tovim* and other mitzvos. It was all very interesting to him.

Alexander also did the shopping for Mother since she found it hard to go up and down the steps of their apartment building. It was a good arrangement and lasted until Father passed away.

The Last Battle

It was the winter of 1993. My father was eighty-three years old, and my mother was eighty-six. One night Father got out of bed and shuffled into the dining room. He may have bumped into the table or he may have just slipped, but suddenly my mother heard him cry out in pain. She found him lying on the floor, unable to get up.

"Mechele, what happened?"

He moaned in response.

"Let me help you get up," she said. He made no effort to do so. He was obviously in a lot of pain, since he could only moan.

Mother called Magen David Adom, the Israeli equivalent of the Red Cross. They arrived quickly and examined my father. The paramedics thought he had broken his hip and took him that night to Hadassah Ein Karem Hospital.

My father did break his hip bone. Recuperation would take a long time. How would my mother be able to deal with Father's situation herself? Chavi lived in Bayit Vegan and took off from work during the various crises my father went through. But the burden on her was becoming overwhelming. Abby came over from England to do her part. She stayed for three weeks, then Boruch came from the United States to relieve her and she went home. Then I came from the States to relieve Boruch. My plan was to stay for three weeks, but I would extend my stay if necessary. I was in a position to stay longer than the others because I was not working at the time.

After a short stay at Hadassah, my father was transferred to Herzog Hospital, more commonly known as Ezrat Nashim. It was a combination rehabilitation and psychiatric hospital and was not equipped to deal with true hospital situations nor with surgery. The administrator of my father's ward, Dr. Wertman,* was a wonderful man, and he tried his best to help my father, but his condition really warranted a fully equipped hospital.

My father was confined to bed part of the day. The other part of the day he was settled in a chair since it was important for him to sit up. He was very disoriented. He did not understand why he was there and wanted to go home. Yisrael Silverman and other grandsons stayed with him in the hospital, because he was so confused. Yisrael heard him cry out numerous times, "*Ribbono shel olam*, help me!" No matter what his situation was, he always felt that he was not alone, that Hashem was with him.

Yisrael observed my father singing Shabbos *zemiros* out loud and sometimes just humming the tune. He did this on Shabbos and also on the weekdays. Sometimes he continued for so long that other patients complained. Singing Shabbos *zemiros* helped him connect to Hashem, to calm himself down, and to give himself encouragement.

For Shabbos we arranged that one of the grandsons sleep over. Sometimes we had the men take turns staying overnight during the week, depending on how my father was feeling. My children came in from Bnei Brak for their shift, which made things more difficult. Sometimes we were short of men, and we called on Alexander and even some of Father's nephews. Occasionally we asked Avrumi Nadav to stay over Shabbos in the hospital.

One Shabbos Avrumi stayed in the hospital with my son Ovadya. My father was still able to speak at that time. He complained about his pain and said he wished everything would be over already. Avrumi tried to reassure him.

With Hashem's help, he was able to calm him down. Father said to Avrumi in Yiddish, "You're such a smart fellow," and then said, "The redemption should come already."

Avrumi answered that he should have a *refuah sheleimah* and that the *yeshua* should come to all of *klal Yisrael*. Father corrected Avrumi and said with a promise, "No, but for you there will be a *yeshua*!"

On *motza'ei Shabbos* Avrumi had to leave. He approached the bed, saying, "*Shavua tov,* Dod Mechele. You should have a *gutte voch* and a *gezunte voch* — a good week and a healthy week."

Father answered, "Soon there will be a week of *yeshuos*, salvations."

"Yes, your *refuah sheleimah* and a *refuah* for everyone," Avrumi responded, thinking that was what he meant.

Avrumi was in the middle of a *shidduch*, and during that

week they decided to become engaged. As soon as they finalized the *shidduch*, Avrumi immediately thought of what my father had told him in the hospital, that his *yeshua* would soon come. When he told his *kallah* about this incident, she was amazed.

Normally, whenever I came to Eretz Yisrael for a visit, it was for a joyous occasion or just to spend time with my married children and grandchildren. When my turn came to be with my father, I stepped off the plane in trepidation. How would I find Deddy? What could I do to help improve his situation? How would my family fend for themselves while I was away? How was my mother taking the strain of this prolonged crisis?

I arrived on Wednesday, December 14, 1993. The next morning I went to Yerushalayim to see my father in Ezrat Nashim Hospital. He was in a good mood.

"When did you come, Perele?" he asked me.

"Yesterday." I kissed him on the cheek. "How are you feeling?"

"Not too bad," he replied. "How long are you staying?"

"For a few weeks." My intention was to remain about three or four weeks. My husband had said he could manage on the home front for that long. Little did we know just how long I would be away from home.

We took my father in a wheelchair to sit outside in the fresh air. He was happy to see me but soon began complaining about the hospital; he did not understand why he could not go home. I tried to make him understand that his bone was broken, and he could not walk or even stand on his legs. I explained that he had an infection and needed medication. He wasn't really hearing me. He was extremely upset at being confined and incapacitated. It was sad to see him in such a state, a man whose whole life had been governed by his drive and vigor to do the will of Hashem.

On one occasion when I came to visit, I found him sitting in a wheelchair near his bed. I asked him if he wanted his tallis with which to daven. He said he did. I put the tallis over his shoulders and draped his head with it. He began davening *shacharis* by heart and closed his eyes to concentrate better. He davened for a very long time, fingering the edge of the tallis lovingly. It made a beautiful picture. I had my camera with me and was tempted to photograph this poignant scene, but I hesitated. He was so intent on his prayers, so deeply in communion with his Maker, that I felt almost like an intruder. To take a photograph at this moment would have somehow cheapened the experience, like a tourist snapping a photo of an interesting sight. For several moments I debated with myself and in the end decided against doing it.

The image of my father in his tallis is clearly etched in my mind. The spiritual glow on his face, the inspiration he aroused at that moment, I would not forget, whether I had the photo or not.

Alexander came that afternoon. Later on he told me that he had sung and danced for Father together with another Russian man, and my father clapped his hands in rhythm. Alexander was so happy to see my father like that.

By then my father had been in the hospital for over a month. For the next four months he went through one crisis after another. He was always running a fever, sometimes quite high. This was a puzzle to the doctors, because he was receiving high doses of antibiotics. And so from time to time we called in a private doctor for a consultation.

On one such occasion, the professor said to us, "Hope for the best, but prepare for the worst." When my father was in septic shock with major organ failure, Abby, Boruch, and Esti came from overseas to see him before it would no longer be possible to do so. Miraculously he pulled through the various crises, and he was shuffled back and forth between Hadassah and Ezrat Nashim.

The mystery of the ongoing fever was finally solved. An abscess was discovered at the site of the fracture. This meant that the area had to be surgically opened and the abscess drained. The doctor said that normally they would not perform surgery on a man of my father's age in his condition, but this infection was life-threatening. The surgery was considered very high-risk, and therefore we hired the surgeon privately to perform it.

The six of us, sisters, brother, sister-in-law, and Mother walked down the long hall alongside Father as he was wheeled to the operating room. He was semiconscious. We huddled around the stretcher, kissing him and giving him our blessings. He opened his eyes for a moment and fixed them on Chavi. He said her name in a broken voice. Then he was taken to surgery, and for the next few hours we did not know if we would see our Deddy again.

We spent those hours in a crowded waiting room with Jews and Arabs, each immersed in his own suffering, waiting to hear the results of his beloved one's surgery. It was supposed to have been a two-hour surgery, but we spent much longer than two hours saying *tehillim* and waiting. Finally, after about five hours, the doctor came out and said that the surgery had been successful and our father's condition was stable. In a short while they would let us into the recovery room, one at a time, to see him.

Abby and Esti stayed overnight in the recovery room area. The rest of us went home. When Abby went in to see Father in the morning, his eyes were open, and he looked at her.

"How are you, Abidess?" he asked, using his pet name for her.

"I'm fine, Deddy. How are you?"

"*Baruch Hashem*!" he answered.

The next day Father was moved to the orthopedic ward. My father's condition had stabilized, and my three siblings left for home within the next few days. I decided to stay on since I knew Mother could not cope with the situation on her own. I went to the hospital every morning, and she came in the afternoon or vice versa. After a while, I told her to stop visiting every day since she was getting terribly exhausted just by walking the long hospital corridors. She would come on Fridays to visit Father and sometimes during the week. He was semiconscious most of the time. Often he would look at us, but we could not tell if he recognized us. He never spoke or attempted to speak.

The fever stopped and then started up again. The doctors were stymied. They did not know what the source of the fever was. The heavy doses of antibiotics gave him thrush, and the antifungal drug caused abdominal bleeding and vomiting. The truth was that the doctors did not know what to do.

The orthopedic ward did not usually keep patients for long periods of time. Usually the patients stabilized and went home or to rehabilitation centers fairly quickly. My father's situation was different. He needed long-term care and the particular type of care suited for a man of his age. The orthopedic ward of a hospital is not a geriatric ward, and it is not equipped to deal with the specific needs of a geriatric patient. My father was not able to sit up in a chair or even in bed. We got a special air mattress whose function was to prevent bedsores. The nurses came to wash him and to turn him in bed three times a day.

We were under the impression that with the special air mattress and the treatment he was getting on the ward my father would be fine. Unfortunately, this was not the case. Before long he developed bedsores. We had no idea of the severity of this condition. Finally the doctors came to the realization that the fever was caused by the bedsores.

One day the orthopedic surgeon came over to me. "Mrs. Toporowitch, your father needs long-term care, and we are not in the position to provide this for him. I know of a wonderful hospital in Jerusalem that administers long-term care for patients when they are terminal or chronically ill," he told me.

"What is the name of this hospital?" I asked him.

"It is the French Catholic Hospital in the Old City, and it is run by nuns. They provide superb care for their patients."

I looked at Dr. Miller* in amazement.

"How can you even consider such a thing!" I exclaimed. "How would he feel being cared for by nuns while living in Eretz Yisrael? How would he feel being in a room with a crucifix hanging on the wall in the center of Yerushalayim?"

Dr. Miller's response angered me even more.

"He does not hear or see what is going on anyway."

"Dr. Miller, I am quite sure that he does hear and perceive a lot of what is taking place, even though he cannot speak!" I was so insistent in my protest at this abominable idea that Dr. Miller backed off. I asked him to give me time to find another hospital for my father.

I knew that Father was aware of what was going on some of the time by the expression in his eyes. He was not always unconscious. And there were numerous incidents that pointed this out to us. On one occasion Boruch spent Shabbos with my father in the hospital. Boruch was learning *Chumash* next to the bed when Father opened his eyes. Boruch gave him the *Chumash* to hold, and Father's eyes closed. Since he wanted to continue learning, Boruch tried to take the *Chumash* from Father's hand, but he held on with a tight grip. As hard as Boruch pulled on the *Chumash,* he felt Father holding on even tighter. He realized that his father was aware of what he was holding — the holy Torah that had been his companion during the many long and rough years of his life. Boruch left the *Chumash* in his hand.

On another occasion Boruch's son, Yossi, came from the United States to see his grandfather. My father no longer spoke at that point and drifted in and out of consciousness. Yossi spent Shabbos in the hospital with two of his friends, Skolyer chassidim. They had their meals in Father's room and sang *zemiros.* Yossi told us that during *seudah shelishis,* when he and his friends were singing *zemiros,* his *zeidy* started crying. He may not have been able to speak, but he could certainly feel.

Once, when I went to see Father, I brought photos of my children from America. His eyes were open, and I showed them to him. He became very alert, looking intently at the pictures, trying perhaps to figure out who the children were. I told him the name of each one and short anecdotes about them. He focused intently on the pictures until he got tired and closed his eyes.

I knew without a doubt that my father would suffer intensely and needlessly if he would be moved to a Catholic hospital to be taken care of by nuns. My job now was to find a suitable place to have him transferred to.

I began making inquiries. Shaare Zedek Hospital in Yerushalayim had a geriatric ward, but the department head did not agree to have Father transferred to his hospital. I then discovered that Tel HaShomer Sheba Hospital in Ramat Gan had an excellent geriatric ward. The administrator was (coincidentally) Dr. Rabinowitz. I contacted him, and he agreed to come to Hadassah to examine my father in order to approve the transfer.

Upon his examination, he saw that my father was in a very serious state of health and had been pitifully neglected. He believed that a person should be given proper respect right up to the moment of his death. He agreed to have Father transferred to his hospital. We felt very grateful to this compassionate man, a special and unique individual. Only later would we understand that he had no hope of saving my father's life. He simply wanted to give him the best medical care that he possibly could as long as he was still with us.

Once Father was transferred to Tel HaShomer I was very pleased with the wonderful care he was now receiving. Its policies included turning immobile patients every two hours versus three times a day in Hadassah. I felt encouraged.

My unmarried sons were in the United States, and I found it hard to ask my married son to spend the whole Shabbos in the hospital, especially since there was so much work to do now that Pesach was approaching. I decided to walk over from Bnei Brak, have *seudah shelishis* there, and ride home on *motza'ei Shabbos*. My father would be alone until I would get there Shabbos afternoon. Just in case, the hospital had the phone number of my son Itzie, where I normally stayed.

Before leaving the hospital, I spoke to a woman I had met whose husband was a patient on the ward. She invited me to sleep with her in a room she rented on the hospital grounds for the duration of Shabbos. I told her that I was spending Shabbos with my mother in Bnei Brak and would walk over during the day. We all wished our silent father a good Shabbos and left. When I got to Bnei Brak, I asked my son-in-law David to walk with me to the hospital on Shabbos afternoon.

My mother and I decided to spend this Shabbos with my daughter Shainy. After the turbulence of that week and the distress we felt over my father's condition, it was good to usher in the Shabbos. Mother and I stood a long time over the Shabbos candles, pouring out our hearts to our Father in Heaven as Jewish women have done over the centuries.

After lighting the candles, I prepared to settle down into the comfortable peace of the Shabbos. But I felt uneasy. I kept thinking to myself that I had made a mistake and should have stayed in the hospital over Shabbos. I kept thinking about the woman's invitation for me to share her room and how I hadn't had the sense to accept her offer. I kept thinking of how alone my Deddy must be feeling with only strangers around him and no one to sing *zemiros* for him. The thoughts nagged at me and gave me no peace.

My mother was enjoying Shabbos with the grandchildren and great-grandchildren, and they were enjoying her. I did not want to disturb her *oneg Shabbos* by saying anything. But by morning I had decided that I would go immediately after the morning meal to the hospital. As soon as we finished the meal and my mother was settled in her room for a nap, I left.

It was a cloudy day, and it rained on and off. I walked fast and kept my mind busy by singing *zemiros* to myself and reciting *tehillim*. Finally I walked into the ward and made my way to my father's room. The nurse stopped me and said, "I'm sorry to tell you that we found your father last night after he was already gone."

Her words did not quite penetrate. I looked at her in amazement.

"What time did it happen?"

"We don't know exactly when he passed away. We called you last night as soon as we found him, but no one answered the phone."

"I spent Shabbos at the home of my daughter," I explained. "Had I heard the phone ringing on Shabbos, maybe I would have walked over last night."

Suddenly the impact of my loss hit me. I turned away from the nurse and rushed off to my father's room, thinking that perhaps he was still there. I looked at the empty bed and burst into tears. I sat down on a chair and sobbed quietly, holding my head in my hands.

It had actually happened. The invincible fighter was finally overcome! And what a fighter he had been. Even in a semiconscious state he had fought. How many times had the doctors told us that the end was near? When he survived each crisis, the doctors were amazed, expressing their wonder that he had pulled through. We came to think that nothing would get him. But now...

The date was 29 Adar 5754 (April 1994). It was Shabbos

and Yom Kippur Katan (when the day before Rosh Chodesh falls on a weekday, it is a day of repentance, a mini Yom Kippur).

The nurse came into the room and put her arms around me. "It's Shabbos," she said. "One is not supposed to mourn on Shabbos."

I knew she was right. But I was overcome and couldn't help myself. I thought of the stories of tzaddikim in which they held back their grief on Shabbos in a superhuman fashion. I understood their greatness better as I struggled unsuccessfully with my feelings. I cried some more, but eventually got control of myself.

"Where is he?" I asked. "I want to go to him."

"That is impossible, dear. No one will give you permission for that, and no one will take you there." The nurse spoke kindly but firmly.

I was not sure of the halachah, but I knew that someone must watch over the body until the time of burial. Also, I knew that in Eretz Yisrael it was common practice to perform autopsies on dead people for their body parts. I was afraid that if I was not there to watch his body I might be negligent in my last duty to my beloved Deddy. But I could not get anywhere with this nurse, and I certainly had no strength to fight for my rights.

"Come and have a cup of hot tea. You must be terribly tired from your walk in the rain." The nurse was trying her best to make me feel better.

I was in a dilemma and did not know what to do. After finishing the tea, I decided to go back to Bnei Brak to my son Itzie. He would go to our *rav* and ask him what to do.

After thanking the nurses for their dedicated care of my

father, I left. It was still raining lightly. The rain felt cool and calmed me down somewhat. I could not believe what had happened. I could not believe that I would not have an opportunity to see my Deddy once again before our last goodbye. I was feeling guilty for not having spent Shabbos with him in the hospital. I was also feeling like a fool for not having understood what the doctors had been trying to tell me all along. And I was wondering how I would face my mother.

The walk took over an hour. I was glad. It allowed me to release some of the tension I was feeling before I faced my family.

I arrived at Itzie's house and walked in. He looked at me and asked me where I was coming from.

"From the hospital."

"What happened?" he asked me. He could see that something was wrong, especially since I had walked back before the end of Shabbos. I was wet and probably looked worn and pale.

I sat down and rested my head on my arms on the dining-room table. I could not say the words, but he understood.

"The phone was ringing at about two o'clock last night. We thought it must have been the hospital. When was he *niftar*?"

"They don't know exactly when it happened. They found him when they came to do a routine checkup. I wanted to go to him, but they didn't let me. What should we do now? Shouldn't someone be there with him?"

"I'll go and ask," Itzie said. He put on his coat and went immediately to ask our *rav* what we should do.

My daughter-in-law, Chaya, brought me something to eat, but I could not eat anything. I felt exhausted, but waited up for Itzie to come back from speaking to our *rav*.

Finally he returned.

"HaRav Chaim said that since he was *niftar* so many hours ago, and he was an old and sick man when he died, we don't have to worry about them removing organs for transplants. And since it is so close to the end of Shabbos anyway, we can wait at home. As soon as Shabbos is over, I will go there and make arrangements with the *chevrah kaddisha.*"

I decided that I would rest a bit and then walk over with Chaya to Shainy's house. We would time it so that we would get there exactly when Shabbos was over. Then I would break the news to my mother.

It took us about twenty minutes to get there. I walked into the house and went over to my mother. She looked at me.

"What is it?" Mother asked, alarmed. "Why didn't you wait until *motza'ei Shabbos* to ride back?"

I couldn't say anything. The expression on my face must have said it all. She understood that Father was no longer with us. She burst into tears and I along with her. We held on to each other, crying on each other's shoulders. Shainy and her children joined us in the dining room, standing around, not knowing what to do. After a while we calmed down, and Mother wanted to know what had happened. I made her sit down and told her the little bit that I knew.

"Itzie is going to the hospital and will watch over the body," I told her. "He is going to speak to the *chevrah kaddisha.*"

Avreimy, Shainy's husband, came home from shul and made Havdalah. My mother wanted me to call her nephew Reb Boruch Leifer. He had moved to Eretz Yisrael years earlier and had kept in touch with my parents since then. Ever since my father had been hospitalized he had been very concerned, calling my mother often to hear how things were. He had been to the hospital a short while before Father passed away. I called my cousin and told him the sad news. He immediately called Itzie, since he wanted to be involved in the final proceedings for the burial, the *chesed shel emes.*

Since it was still Shabbos in the United States, we only called Boruch seven hours later. He said he did not want us to delay the *levayah* until he could get there. It was decided that the *levayah* would take place the following day at ten o'clock. Our *rav* felt that it would be a very small *levayah* if we would make it that night, and for my father's honor we should have more people there. Mother and I also spoke to Abby in England.

Avreimy decided to join Itzie for the overnight vigil. Early in the morning they would take the body to the funeral home in Yerushalayim, where the *taharah* would be done. We followed later by van. It was still raining and gray outside. The weather suited our mood perfectly.

My father passed away ten days after entering Tel HaShomer Hospital. His last days there were days of true caring for the patient and consideration for the family members. We will forever be grateful to Dr. Rabinowitz for his outstanding concern and treatment of our father.

Ironically, two days earlier, on Thursday, Father's older sister Surale Arak had passed away. None of us knew about it. She was brought to Israel for burial and taken to the same funeral home that my father was taken to. She had been buried on Har HaZeisim on Friday. When we got there and walked into the place, there was a sign up on the wall announcing the passing of my aunt. My mother never even noticed it, nor did I. Only Hashem knows why the passing of a sister and brother occurred so close to each other and only a few days after their father's *yahrtzeit* on the twenty-fourth of Adar.

The Levayah

When we got to the funeral home, someone cut the front of our blouses for the *kriah*; I can't even remember who it was. We were told to ask forgiveness from the *niftar.* Chavi and I held on to Mother as we approached the still shape wrapped in a tallis.

No longer would we see his smiling face. No longer would he make jokes and worry about our welfare. No longer would he sing his *zemiros* and talk to his Creator. No longer would he give people encouragement with his words and his charity. No longer... But such is the way of the flesh. Hashem gives life and Hashem takes life. We said our last words and prayers silently to him. Mother was very broken, and she remained bent over in submission to her loss for a long time.

Since it was Rosh Chodesh, no *hespedim* were said. Reb Boruch Leifer just said some *divrei Torah* of my father's. I was not able to concentrate and so remember none of it. He told us later that at home, prior to the *levayah,* he had opened up my father's *sefer, Zimras HaAretz.* It opened to *parashas Vayikra,* the parashah of that week. The words he read fit perfectly with what he wanted to say about my father.

The custom in Yerushalayim is that the women do not go to the cemetery. We were dropped off in Bayit Vegan while people from there joined the procession. We went upstairs to my parents' apartment. It wouldn't be the same for me ever again.

The Shivah

Boruch joined us in the middle of the *shivah*. Abby could not come since her husband had suffered a heart attack at just about the same time. My girls took turns coming in from Bnei Brak to prepare meals for us.

Boruch decided to give our father's *sefer* to the men who came to be *menacheim avel*. Rav Chaim Greineman came from Bnei Brak, and upon examining the *sefer* and seeing what my father had written in the flyleaf, that the author was giving it away for free and wanted no reimbursement for it, exclaimed, "I never saw such a thing. Never." He was impressed that a person would spend his own money to publish words of Torah for the sake of Heaven.

Many of the people who came to comfort us knew our father only in his older, more subdued years. Invariably we kept hearing that they were impressed with him as a person who was always smiling and always happy. One man said that even though things were really hard for Reb Mechel he always smiled. He took life as it was, and he didn't let anything get him down. You could see in him the fire within that kept him going.

I mentioned to a friend of mine that I was upset that I hadn't been in the hospital that last Shabbos and that my father had been alone. She told me that it is written that when the family members are nearby, sometimes it is hard for the *neshamah* to leave and make its final transition. She said that when her son was very close to leaving this world, both she and her husband were there with him in the hospital room, but they had both fallen asleep. They awoke only after he was gone. She said that they, too, felt terrible at the turn of events until someone said this to them. Sometimes the family members can't be around at the time of the *petirah*. Ironically Father felt the same when his brother the Skolyer Rebbe was *niftar*.

Reb Velvel comforted us by saying that this world was missing people like our father. He was "*malei v'gadush*," full to overflowing. He was serious and sincere in his *Yiddishkeit*.

After the Shivah

Friday, a short while before Shabbos, we got up from the *shivah* and made our Shabbos preparations. We had a somber Shabbos together, but I can't remember any details of it. Since Boruch and I were going home very shortly after the *shivah*, the tombstone had been ordered and was ready to be erected on Sunday.

We went to the grave site on Har HaZeisim with Reb Boruch Leifer, Reb Velvel Gottlieb, some of the *kollel* men, and some of my children, enough to make a minyan. We recited *tehillim*, and Boruch said Kaddish. We each said our own private prayers while we were there. The tombstone recorded some of Father's *yichus* (genealogy) and some of the things he had done in his lifetime. We faced the Har Habayis, the Temple Mount, and prayed that the *geulah* should come quickly.

The next day, Monday, I flew home alone. I hadn't really assimilated all that had happened. I arrived home on the tenth of Nissan, a few days before Pesach. I would need all of my strength for the final preparations before the holiday.

My daughters and daughters-in-law had cleaned the house and started the cooking, but I would have to finish off the cooking and do the last-minute shopping. It was good to be busy. It was good to be home. I had been away for the last three and a half months. It felt like a lifetime. So much had happened in those few months, and life would never be the same again. The comfort of home was invaluable.

Boruch felt that Mother should come with him to the States for Pesach. She wasn't keen on the idea, but she agreed to come. She made the *sedarim* in Boro Park with Boruch's family. Afterward she came to visit us in Monsey. While she was with us, I took her and the children to a beautiful park. The children fed the geese, and Mother enjoyed watching them. I wanted her to relax as much as possible before she went back. And she was impatient to get back, for she loved her home in Eretz Yisrael.

Life would be different for her now, but home was where she wanted to be. Being on her own at her age would be no simple matter. My father's essence saturated her home, and she had lived with him for nearly fifty-four years. But if there was one thing she had learned living with my father all those years, it was that Hashem was always with her.